THE BEST GIFT
MONTANA'S CARNEGIE LIBRARIES

Kate Hampton

photographs by Tom Ferris

ISBN: 978-1-59152-250-8

Furthermore:
a program of the J.M. Kaplan Fund

Generous funding from Furthermore: a program of the J. M. Kaplan Fund
supported the printing and binding of this book.

M+F

THE MONTANA HISTORY
F O U N D A T I O N

Published by The Montana History Foundation
1750 North Washington Street
Helena, MT 59601; (406) 449-3770

sweetgrassbooks
an imprint of Farcountry Press

Produced by Sweetgrass Books; Distributed by Farcountry Press
PO Box 5630, Helena, MT 59604; (800) 821-3874;
www.sweetgrassbooks.com

Library of Congress Cataloging-in-Publication Data

Names: Hampton, Kate, 1969- author.
Title: The best gift : Montana's Carnegie libraries / by Kate Hampton ;
    photography by Tom Ferris.
Description: Helena, MT : Montana History Foundation, 2019. | Includes
    bibliographical references. | Summary: "An illustrated history of
    Montana's Carnegie Libraries"-- Provided by publisher.
Identifiers: LCCN 2019023957 | ISBN 9781591522508 (hardcover)
Subjects: LCSH: Carnegie libraries--Montana--History--20th century. |
    Public libraries--Montana--History--20th century.
Classification: LCC Z732.M9 H36 2019 | DDC 027.409786--dc23
LC record available at https://lccn.loc.gov/2019023957

Printed in the United States of America.

24   23   22   21   20   2   3   4   5   6

TABLE OF CONTENTS

ACKNOWLEDGMENTS

Andrew Carnegie famously said that a "library outranks any one thing a community can do to benefit its people." Because of his vision and generosity, generations of Montanans have benefitted from his libraries.

This project was inspired by Penelope Wilson, who not only came up with the idea, but like Carnegie, donated the funds to get it started. The Donnelley Foundation and dozens of individual donors also contributed generously to the project. We are grateful to all of them.

Creating the book was a collaborative effort, and we are fortunate to have had the assistance of State Librarian Jennie Stapp and librarians from all seventeen original Carnegie library communities around the state. Behind them stand generations of librarians who dedicated their lives and careers to providing Montanans free and public access to libraries. We thank them all.

Many thanks are due to Mary Greenfield, who spent countless hours at Columbia University researching the Carnegie collections and collecting Montana references; Helena-based historian Patty Dean; and the Montana Historical Society staff for their invaluable research support. Tom Ferris was accompanied on his many photographic journeys by his wife Taylor and their dog Chin. Sprinkled among Tom's contemporary images are historical images researched and identified by Becca Kohl. Thanks also to John Clayton, Suzy Hampton, and H.D. Hampton, who read and provided helpful feedback on earlier versions of the manuscript. Finally, Charlene Porsild and the amazing team at the Montana History Foundation coordinated every piece of the project, taking it from the original idea and shepherding it through to the final product. We hope you enjoy reading it as much as we enjoyed creating it.

FOREWORD

IT WOULD NOT BE AN EXAGGERATION TO SAY THAT MY life has been a series of libraries.

First, in Ashland, Oregon—where I'd walk to the Carnegie library after grade school each day, immersing myself in books about dinosaurs and UFOs, until my mom would pick me up an hour later.

Then when a book was banned from my junior high, I immediately went to the public library, found it and read it. That book inspired me to become a writer myself.

In high school, the first time I ever skipped school, I went to the public library. Libraries were always a place of enlightenment, possibility, and hope, and at times my sanctuary.

So it was no surprise when I met my wife at (you guessed it) the public library.

Now as a bestselling author, I am privileged to visit libraries all over the country—many of them Carnegie libraries. I'm always impressed with the timelessness of these places that are still so important to the communities they serve, especially here in Montana. One day I hope to visit them all.

In the meantime, there's this book, which like all great books, will take you there from the comfort of your favorite reading chair.

I hope you enjoy the journey.

Jamie Ford
Great Falls, Montana
New York Times bestselling author of
Hotel on the Corner of Bitter and Sweet

MONTANA'S CARNEGIE LIBRARIES

Havre • • Chinook

Malta • • Glasgow

Kalispell •

Fort Benton •

Great Falls •

Lewistown •

Missoula •

Miles City •

Hamilton •

Big Timber •

Bozeman • Hardin •

Livingston •

Dillon • Red Lodge •

INTRODUCTION

Montanans love their libraries. They visit libraries to learn and to be entertained. Libraries allow people to connect with their neighbors, with the world, and with their own imaginations. Today, Montana counts more than one hundred public and branch libraries. The building of their presence across the state took determination and strong local investment. That alone, however, was not always enough. Between 1901 and 1922, seventeen Montana communities received gifts from the wealthiest man in the world, Andrew Carnegie, to construct their libraries. Most of these buildings continue to serve their patrons as libraries, while others have been adapted for use as cultural centers or offices. The fifteen Carnegie libraries that remain standing in Montana are important touchstones for their communities.

The Birth of Montana's Carnegie Libraries

Thirteen-year-old Andrew Carnegie and his family left their native Scotland and arrived in Allegheny City (now part of Pittsburgh), Pennsylvania in 1848. He found employment at a cotton factory first as a bobbin boy, then as an engineer's assistant, responsible for stoking the boilers and running the engine in the cellar for twelve hours a day, six days a week. On Saturdays, Carnegie found respite and inspiration in a local private library. Businessman and iron manufacturer Colonel James Anderson offered his collection of 400 books to working boys to use, and this generosity had a lasting impact on Carnegie.

The ambitious Carnegie worked hard, became a superintendent for the Pennsylvania Railroad by his early twenties, and invested his money wisely in materials and

▲ A library float in the Fort Benton Parade, ca. 1920.

industry. He turned to the steel industry in the 1870s, and by 1892 his Carnegie Steel Company was one of the most influential and successful enterprises in the world. Carnegie believed that the rich had a responsibility to give away their wealth in a way that promoted "real and permanent good in this world" and helped people help themselves. His visits to Colonel Anderson's library as a youth influenced his decision to fund libraries—he determined that a library constituted "the best gift" to give to a community.

In 1883, Carnegie funded construction of a free public library in his birthplace, Dunfermline, Scotland. Next, he funded libraries in southwest Pennsylvania, the place where he earned his fortune. Expanding his sphere of generosity, he began to fund additional locales in 1898. Over the next twenty-four years, just six states—

Indiana, California, Ohio, New York, Illinois, and Iowa—accounted for more than one-third of the 1,689 Carnegie-funded library buildings across the country. Montana's seventeen Carnegie gifts were about average for the remaining states and territories.

At first, the funding process was relatively simple. A community wrote to Andrew Carnegie and requested money to build a library. The inquiry needed only to state the town's population, a commitment to secure building lots, and a promise to pay to maintain the library into the future. Carnegie routinely gave at least $2 per resident for construction, and often more.

Few specific architectural requirements accompanied the funding. In Montana, the eight Carnegie libraries completed between 1902 and 1907 reflected this relative freedom of design. Dillon (1902) and Lewistown (1907) both incorporated exuberant stone edifices featuring local materials and craftsmanship. Architect Charles Haire's monumental designs for Miles City (1903), Great Falls (1903), and Bozeman (1904), along with George Shanley's drawings for Kalispell (1904), embraced high-style elements, including domes, stone columns, deep, dentiled overhangs, and highly decorative cornices. In Missoula (1904) and Livingston (1904), the Neoclassical Revival-style libraries included grandly scaled entries and windows.

By 1906, Andrew Carnegie's library program and his other charitable projects consumed so much of his time that he turned increasingly to his longtime personal secretary, James Bertram, to handle the details of the program. Bertram created a stricter set of procedures for applicants, with specific language for communities to use when establishing their local library funds and accepting the Carnegie gift. Bertram also created guidelines for library design that favored simpler yet dignified construction and emphasized usable space and efficiency. In 1911, Carnegie formed the Carnegie Corporation of New York to officially administer his charitable endeavors, and chose Bertram as the corporation's founding secretary. That year, Bertram began to distribute his "Notes on the Erection of Library Bildings" (*sic*), which offered sample floor plans for small and medium-sized libraries.

Bertram's new guidelines required a single point of contact between himself and the community, verifiable population numbers, and draft architectural drawings for his review. Nine Montana communities proved themselves willing and able to meet these requirements. Following these exacting procedures generally resulted in more correspondence and longer periods of negotiation between the corporation and applicants. Each of the

▲ Architect George Shanley's original design for the Kalispell Carnegie Library featured a large central dome. Budget constraints required Shanley to redesign the building with a smaller domed entry instead.

libraries of Montana's second wave displayed the architectural restraint advocated by Bertram, often necessitated by the cost and availability of materials.

Beginning with the library at Glasgow, Montana (1909), these Carnegie libraries featured brick veneer exteriors, centered entries set off by pilasters or columns, rectangular footprints, flat or hipped roofs, modest cornices, and single stories atop daylight basements—the elements that became the hallmarks of the "Carnegie Classic" architectural style. Main floors contained a central circulation desk, stacks, and reading rooms, while the basements housed space for an assembly or lecture room with separate access from the main entry. Mechanical rooms and restrooms were typically also located in the basement. These common elements make the Carnegie

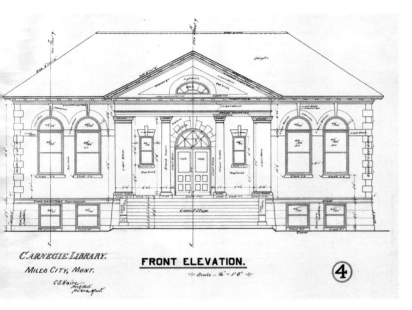

CARNEGIE LIBRARY.

MILES CITY, MONT.

C.S.Haire
Architect
Helena, Mont.

FRONT ELEVATION.

Scale: 1/4" = 1'0"

④

▲ Architect Charles S. Haire designed Montana's first three Carnegie libraries: Dillon, Miles City, and Great Falls. IMAGE COURTESY OF MSU-BOZEMAN, 2040-F103-005

libraries built between 1909 and 1922 easily recognizable, and they stand as important visual landmarks in their communities' civic landscapes.

▮ Early Libraries in Montana

Because of their size, weight, and susceptibility to the elements, books were relatively rare and highly prized commodities in Montana during the nineteenth and early twentieth centuries. Though texts were cumbersome, Meriwether Lewis and William Clark traveled through the region with a library of scientific tomes, reference books, a history of Louisiana, and maps essential to their Corps of Discovery's success. Other explorers and fur traders also carried valued volumes with them or sought them out when they came to the territory. One of Montana's

very first libraries was at Fort McKenzie, near present-day Loma. Between 1833 and 1844, this collection "contain[ed] a little of everything, science, history, poetry and fiction." In 1861, the Stuart brothers rode 150 miles from the Deer Lodge Valley to the Bitterroot to purchase books from a collection there. Two years later, John Mullan described the book collection at Fort Owen as "the finest [he had] seen on the north Pacific coast."

As elsewhere in the United States, Montana's first libraries were accessed through membership or subscriptions. One of the first publicly accessible subscription libraries opened in Helena in 1868. Wrote one Helena resident, "Here where the allurements to vice are many, and intellectual entertainments few; where hundreds of men have leisure, and little acquaintance, and the gratification of their desire to read [is] otherwise expensive, the establishment of a circulating Library and the maintenance of cheerful reading rooms . . . is fraught with manifold benefits to the entire community."

Fort Benton and Deer Lodge soon followed, and Bozeman called for a public library in 1872. As the population increased over the next several decades, community leaders across the territory established libraries. These institutions (often simply a room in a private home) offered educational opportunities in the hope that young men would find them a suitable alternative to saloons, gambling houses, and brothels. Local residents also believed that libraries might bring increased stability to their community.

The 1883 Montana Territorial Legislative Assembly empowered cities and towns to levy up to a one mill tax—$1 for every $1,000 of property value—to "establish and maintain one free public library for the use of [its] citizens." Subsequently, several cities, including Helena,

Butte, Dillon, Great Falls, Bozeman, and Glasgow, established library funds through taxation. While these monies allowed for acquisition and maintenance of books, most communities lacked the means to construct a dedicated library building. There were exceptions: the William H. Kohrs Memorial Library in Deer Lodge, the Hearst Free Library in Anaconda, the Butte Public Library, and the Parmly Billings Memorial Library were all built with the infusion of funds from wealthy local benefactors. Other towns, however, housed their collections in cramped city halls or rented rooms. Dillon's library existed in "a miserable wooden shack," while at the Hamilton library the smells from the livery next door proved offensive.

By 1900, the pressing need for dedicated library buildings coincided with the rise of Progressive Era social organizations, a wave of new municipalities, and the availability of construction funds from Andrew Carnegie. In Montana, as in other states, women's clubs took up the task. Nationally, women's clubs had their origins as literary societies, and advocating for libraries was a natural extension of their mission. This was true in Montana, where formal and informal groups of women, from Missoula to Miles City and numerous communities in between, established book collections and reading rooms. As Montana's population mushroomed, these endeavors intersected with local governments' desire to establish attractive civic institutions to bolster a sense of permanence. Andrew Carnegie's library program, dedicated to "promot[ing] the advancement and diffusion of knowledge and understanding among the people of

▲ Women's clubs influenced many communities' efforts to obtain funding to build a Carnegie library. The Fort Benton Women's Club, pictured here in 1900, was also instrumental in pushing for statewide legislation to establish free public libraries across the state.

the United States," proved well-suited to accomplishing these goals.

In Montana, the mid-1910s witnessed dramatic population increases, especially in the eastern part of the state, attributable to the opening of reservation lands to non-Indian settlement, boosterism, and the passage of the Enlarged Homestead Act of 1909. The Montana Library Association (MLA), established in 1906, promoted libraries in these areas. The 1915 county library law allowed residents to petition their county governments to levy up to two mills to maintain a library. Spearheaded by Gertrude Buckhous, the university librarian in Missoula and a MLA

▲ Andrew Carnegie did not require that his name be placed on the exterior of the library buildings he funded, though many communities chose to honor him in that way such as this one in Havre.

leader, the law gave Montana counties the authority to apply for Carnegie funds for the first time. Dedicated to the county library program's success and its potential to reach rural Montanans, Buckhous sometimes intervened with Bertram on the applicant's behalf. Bertram respected her professional expertise and not only welcomed but also sought out her opinions and explanations.

◼ A Century of Service

The flurry of settlement and construction that defined much of Montana history through the late nineteenth and early twentieth centuries came to a quick end by the late 1910s, when farmers' fortunes began to turn. Widespread drought began in 1917 and placed enormous strain on the agricultural economy. After World War I ended in 1918, speculative banking practices and the constriction of extractive industries, such as logging and mining, further contributed to the economic crisis in Montana during the 1920s. Montana was the only state to lose population between 1920 and 1930. Dependent on tax revenues, many local libraries struggled to stay fiscally sound through the 1930s.

Despite the challenges, and often with the steady support of local women's clubs, Montana's seventeen Carnegie libraries remained open and steadily increased their collections and outreach efforts. Their services included branch libraries, rural delivery, and special children's programming. During the Great Depression, local public libraries functioned as information hubs where farmers could learn about new agricultural methods and techniques. They also served and continue to serve as community gathering places. (The Fort Benton Women's Club, for example, has met monthly in the basement of the Carnegie library for more than a century.) For rural patrons, the arrival of a book truck or an excursion to the library in town offered respite from troubled times and the opportunity to connect with others.

Montana libraries' fortunes improved with the rest of the economy following World War II. In 1949, the MLA successfully petitioned the legislature to fund the Montana State Library Commission (SLC). The SLC and its team of professional librarians supported local libraries by loaning books, providing field visits and trainings, and responding to librarians' inquiries for help and advice. Still, by 1954, approximately one-fourth of Montana's population of 143,995 people lacked access to library services. That year the legislature authorized a State Library Extension Commission (SLEC) dedicated to founding new libraries, "improving established libraries, and aiding in the establishment of traveling libraries." In Montana, the SLEC administered programs funded in part by the national Library Services Act of 1956, a landmark piece of legislation that offered funding for collections, staff, equipment, interlibrary loans, and bookmobile programs. It also supported the development of library federations, multi-county cooperative organizations that allowed libraries to share resources.

Whereas the Library Services Act significantly helped advance Montana's library programming, the 1964 Library Services and Construction Act stimulated the

▲ Many Carnegie libraries in Montana made use of local materials, such as the Big Timber library's river rock daylight basement, called out by the chalk graffiti here.

▲ Twelve of Montana's fifteen remaining Carnegie libraries are listed in the National Register of Historic Places, either as individual buildings or as part of a historic district, as in Hamilton.

the buildings' original designs and preserved their historic and architectural integrity.

A Living Legacy

Determined efforts by local groups and individuals fostered the construction of Montana's Carnegie libraries. Hazel Allison Pasma of Chinook was one of many women's club members across the state who actively worked to obtain funding from Andrew Carnegie to build a local library. She and her colleagues gathered names on petitions, wrote letters and newspaper articles, fundraised, secured land donations, and encouraged their elected officials to follow through on the applications. Wrote Pasma, "It seemed like a colossal task for such a small group of women to undertake, but we were told by the Foundation, if we would secure a plot of ground, and a means of support, maintenance, etc. after it was built, they would put up a building for us."

Likewise, women's clubs, librarians, community leaders, donors, voters, builders, and architects worked together to construct seventeen Carnegie public libraries across Montana between 1902 and 1922. Today, Montana's fifteen surviving Carnegie library buildings represent the long-term commitment to education, social improvement, and civic responsibility of its early citizens. Nine of Montana's Carnegie libraries continue to serve their communities as public libraries; three provide an alternative cultural experience as art venues; two contribute to their locality by providing office space; while one awaits rehabilitation. These Carnegie libraries stand as cultural and architectural reminders that local history is connected to statewide and national events, programs, and trends while also reflecting their communities' identity and our common heritage.

physical transformation of many of the state's libraries, including those originally constructed with Carnegie support. The federal program provided matching funds to materially increase and improve libraries' capacity to serve. Miles City and Custer County took advantage of the program in 1965 to pay for an extensive remodel and addition to their original 1903 Carnegie building. The same year, Glasgow and Great Falls both demolished their Carnegie libraries and constructed new facilities. By 1981, Kalispell, Missoula, Malta, Chinook, and Bozeman had abandoned their Carnegies for new accommodations. The remaining eight Carnegie libraries underwent upgrades, expanding collections and programming, improving accessibility, building additions, and accommodating new technologies. Many of these changes were respectful of

▲ Carnegie libraries continue to serve as community meeting places. Here, United States Senator Jon Tester takes a turn behind the reference desk with head librarian Jacque Scott and assistant librarian James Goos before a public meeting at the Big Timber Carnegie Public Library in 2018.

DILLON

Mary Russell Perkins Hooker and her husband, the Reverend Sidney Hooker, arrived in Dillon—a railroad town, agricultural trade center, and county seat—in 1888, just eight years after its founding. From their home in the Episcopal rectory, Mrs. Hooker quickly set out to serve the community, not only as a missionary but also as a cultural ambassador: "The quarter century of Mrs. Hooker's residence in Dillon was a formative period in the history of the town, and there is little vital in the moral, intellectual, or social character of the community today that is not attributable directly or indirectly, in some way or in some degree, to [her] influence."

Raised in Connecticut, she was the great-niece of Harriet Beecher Stowe, the author of *Uncle Tom's Cabin*, and from a young age she was immersed in a rich literary tradition. Together with other community members, the Reverend and Mrs. Hooker founded a book club in 1888, and two years later that club organized an official library association. Members paid a small fee each year to access the collections located in rooms within the Masonic Lodge.

In 1892 the library association voted to eliminate the membership charges and create a truly free public library. Mrs. Hooker organized fundraisers and also worked as a librarian. The library had a minimal budget; volunteers throughout the community provided fuel, maintenance, and space and fulfilled librarian duties. It moved several times between 1891 and 1894, from the Masonic Lodge to a grocery, a bank, and the Episcopal parish house. Reverend Hooker approached the city council in 1896, and the city voted in favor of a levy for library support in April of that year. In September 1897, chief librarian Hooker reported a collection of nearly two thousand volumes.

▲ The Dillon Carnegie library strongly resembles a church.

As the library continued to grow, the need for alternative space became apparent. In November 1901, library trustee Reverend Henry Cotes applied to Carnegie on behalf of the city, explaining that "the books are kept in a miserable wooden shack. . . . We feel keenly that the impression created . . . by the library housed in a hutch is the opposite of the one we seek. . . . Our collection is always in great danger of fire." Because the application process at this early stage of Carnegie library giving required only completion of a questionnaire and a letter of request, Cotes received a swift reply: Carnegie promised $7,500 just two months later. Dillon quickly complied with the conditions of the gift in March 1902 by resolving to provide the land, the books, and the furnishings and to levy at least $750 annually (10 percent of Carnegie's contribution) to maintain the property as a free library.

The city council chose two corner lots offered by A. F. Graeter "in a splendid portion of town, near the business portion, yet not exactly in the business portion . . . as near the center of population as possible." During the early years of the library program, Carnegie and his staff reviewed the designs but did not require specific styles or floor plans, so architect Charles S. Haire and his library committee clients had relatively free rein to design a building that best suited the community. Haire completed the Parmly Billings Memorial Library in 1901 and likely adapted its imposing Romanesque Revival style elements to the smaller scale required in Dillon. Perhaps in honor of Dillon's first library supporters, Haire's asymmetrical design resembled a church, with its steeply pitched roof, octagonal tower, multiple bays at varying depths, and arched entries and windows. He also called for it to be built of rough-faced buff-colored granite quarried from Frying Pan Basin, northwest of the city. George M. Smith of Butte won the construction contract with his bid of $7,300 on July 31, 1902.

Though she remained intimately involved with the library until her husband was reassigned to Helena in 1911, Mrs. Hooker resigned as librarian in 1901 because of ill health, and longtime library volunteer Mary Innes stepped in to take her place. A member of the library building committee, Innes oversaw the transfer of the collection to the new building when major construction was completed on December 22, 1902. The new library opened to the public five days later and contained a reading room, reference room, and children's room, all finished with plaster walls, maple floors, exposed oak trusses, wainscoting, and built-in bookshelves. For the first few weeks, before the light fixtures arrived, it was open only in the afternoon.

Officially named librarian in 1909, Mary Innes also

▲ Montana's first Carnegie library made from Dillon local granite. Charles Haire's Romanesque Revival design included a turret, arched windows, steeply pitched roof lines, and numerous carved stone adornments. IMAGE COURTESY MONTANA HISTORICAL SOCIETY 946-756.

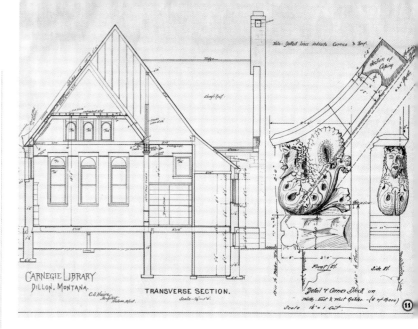

▲ Haire offered very detailed plans for the Dillon library, with numerous carved stone embellishments. IMAGE COURTESY OF MSU-BOZEMAN 2040-F103-011.

taught elementary school in Dillon, having earned her degree in education from the Montana State Normal College and her library training at the University of Chicago and the University of California, Berkeley. She served in this dual capacity through 1938, when she retired from teaching. She worked at the library until her death in 1964. During her tenure, Innes directed the library through nearly continuous growth and innovation. Together with her counterpart, Mrs. John Orr, Innes completed the educational requirements to receive lifetime certification from the Montana Library Association. In 1948, the Dillon library also received accreditation. With a dedicated staff, trustees, and volunteers, the library continued to thrive through the mid-twentieth century. Mrs. Orr

reflected in 1950: "To those who have thought that the remarkable increase in television sets, of movies, of radios, of spectacular sports and the automobile would sound the death knell of book reading as a leisure activity, it should be balm to hear that such seems not to be the case."

At the request of the Dillon library, state librarian Alma Smith Jacobs visited during the early 1970s and made recommendations designed to provide more efficient service and consolidate space. Between 1975 and 1976, a grant and private donations helped fund interior improvements, including additional shelving, carpeting, and displays. These minor changes did not alter the original building significantly. Twenty years later, the first major changes to Dillon's Carnegie library became necessary. The $250,000 rehabilitation, paid for in part by a Library Services and Construction grant, was extensive and respectful to the ninety-seven-year-old building's original

design. To improve accessibility, a ramp was introduced, but it was placed behind ornamental fencing and landscaping to help it blend in. Contractors used original stones found in the building's basement to extend the front entry and deepen the porch. The renovation included finishing the basement level to create meeting rooms, a children's programming space, computer services, and restrooms. At the main level, contractors restored and reintroduced original lighting and refurbished the original fittings. As a result, the thoroughly modern library occupies a fully functional and historic space.

The Dillon Public Library represents one of the community's most enduring institutions. Beginning with a book club's idea in the 1880s, the people of Dillon have supported their library for more than 130 years. Early efforts culminated in Montana's first Carnegie library building to be put into service: Charles Haire's most complete, though relatively diminutive, example of Richardsonian Romanesque design. Loyal and beloved staff and volunteers guided the library through the twentieth and into the twenty-first century by introducing expanded technology and space within the historic walls of their "castle of books."

◄ Dillon's Carnegie library features a complicated, steeply pitched roof. After 1911, most Carnegie libraries reflected a simpler, more uniform style.

▲ Portraits of (left to right) Dillon librarian Mary Innes, Andrew Carnegie, Mary Hooker, and city founder Benjamin White (below) hang in the Dillon Public Library today, reminders of the women and men who helped build Montana's first Carnegie library.

▲ The interior of the Dillon Public Library features multiple arched windows, high beamed ceilings, built-in bookshelves, and ornate light fixtures. Many of these original design elements have been preserved in the modern library's reading room.

MILES CITY

WHEN TEN-YEAR-OLD LAURA MANDERSCHEID Brown arrived in Miles City with her family via steamboat in 1878, she saw a fledgling city of about 150 residents nestled at the confluence of the Yellowstone and Tongue Rivers. Miles City had recently been founded by settlers after its namesake, General Nelson A. Miles, evicted whiskey traders from the nearby Fort Keogh in 1877. Brown's family became an integral part of the fast-growing community through the 1880s. They and other settlers sought to launch institutions familiar to them, including a library.

As in other Montana communities, Miles City's first libraries included private collections and a small "volunteer library" consisting of donated books available for loan. A local group of dedicated women offered a library within a downtown store soon after the town's founding. By 1882, the local newspaper began to call for a more

formal public library and reading room, encouraging the townswomen to "act upon it promptly." Four years later, another library and reading room opened to the public daily from 10 A.M. to 10 P.M. This institution served not only as a source of information and literary enjoyment but also as a space where local citizens might conduct themselves "in a strictly moral manner." In other words, the 1886 Miles City library was established as an alternative to the many local saloons and brothels.

By 1900, Miles City's public reading room had closed, but the local schools maintained a fifteen-hundred-volume library. The new Custer County Ladies Library Auxiliary revived the idea of a free public library and initiated discussion regarding a Carnegie library gift. Encouraged by public feedback, in June 1901 a local attorney named T. J. Porter called upon General Miles to contact Andrew Carnegie on the city's behalf. "I know the people of this

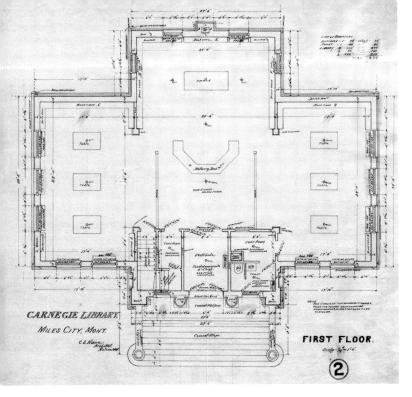

CARNEGIE LIBRARY.
MILES CITY, MONT.

FIRST FLOOR.

②

▲ Haire's floor plan for the Miles City Carnegie library shows the modified cross layout with a large central foyer. IMAGE COURTESY OF MSU-BOZEMAN 0863-F119-004.

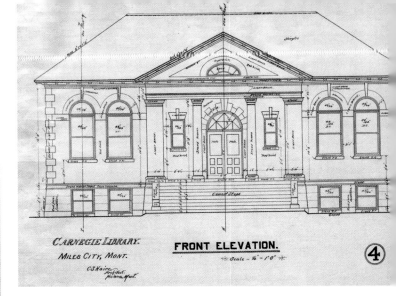

CARNEGIE LIBRARY.
MILES CITY, MONT.

FRONT ELEVATION.

④

▲ The Miles City Public Library, designed by Charles Haire, featured a classically inspired design with arched windows, deep eaves, and stately columns on the wide front entry. IMAGE COURTESY OF MSU-BOZEMAN 0863-F119-004.

town and of the surrounding country, for which it is the intellectual center, to be a people as worthy of his consideration as can be found anyplace on the globe," Porter entreated. Miles heartily endorsed the petition and went so far as to flatter Carnegie's benevolence as "the greatest possible good . . . for the welfare of the human race."

A jubilant Miles City populace received word just a month later, on July 31, that Carnegie approved a $10,000 gift to erect a library in that city—the first Carnegie library monies to be granted in Montana. Within weeks, the residents voted overwhelmingly in favor of accepting the gift and supporting the required $1,000 mill levy. Public subscribers invested an additional $1,000 to

purchase four lots on Main Street near the courthouse. By January 1902, the paper work was in place, and the search for an architect began.

Helena architect Charles Haire had completed the Parmly Billings Memorial Library the previous year. For Miles City he offered a lofty Italian Renaissance Revival design that met with the Miles City library board's favor, but not their pocketbook. At the board's request, Haire revised his vision of a domed, T-shaped building to a substantially smaller, domeless, hip-roofed, modified cross. The redesign he submitted in spring 1902 retained the hallmarks of the Renaissance Revival style, including round-arched windows, a colonnaded entry, a fanlight, and deep, bracketed eaves. The library's rough stone daylight basement featured sandstone from Columbus, Montana, and smooth red-brick upper-story walls. Originally designed with a large closed stack room within

▲ Haire's 1902 design for the Miles City Carnegie library exhibits a balanced, classically influenced, ornate façade. Subsequent Carnegie libraries across Montana were more restrained.
IMAGE COURTESY MONTANA HISTORICAL SOCIETY PAC 2013-50 MICL.

a deep south wing, Haire's modified plans incorporated open stacks and large reading rooms to either side of a central circulation and reference desk. Restricted-access stacks occupied the building's shallow south extension. Construction began in the late summer of 1902. Delays in installing the heating equipment, however, required the community to wait several months before occupation.

The Miles City Public Library, the second Carnegie-funded library in Montana, opened on April 1, 1903. On hand was Laura Manderscheid Brown Zook, the long-time resident who was now the city's librarian. Brown had become a schoolteacher and married another pioneer in the area, Johnny Zook, in 1889. When her husband died just six years later, leaving her with an infant son, she returned to her teaching career and became the superintendent of the

huge Custer County School District. She also took on the role of city librarian, a post she would hold for forty years.

During her tenure, the Custer County Ladies Library Auxiliary, later renamed the Miles City Women's Club, supported Zook's efforts. Their primary mission was to obtain "maximum library facilities for the community." In the 1920s, Zook and the women's club sought to expand the children's department into the "admirably lighted" basement, and Zook wrote to Carnegie Corporation Secretary James Bertram that in doing so, they hoped to "double their good work." The women's club offered innovative strategies for fundraising, and despite drought, economic depression, and bank closures, they succeeded in keeping the library open. Meanwhile, Zook took every opportunity to advocate for the library, including lobbying to maintain Sunday hours and expand its services countywide. Zook retired in 1943 and died a year later. Her coworkers memorialized her as "a power of good in all walks of her life" and further noted that "no woman in the county was better known or held in higher affection and esteem."

By the 1950s, librarian Clare Flynn Smith, together with children's librarian Mildred Myers Schlosser, had built on Zook's mission by offering more programs and services. Schlosser introduced puppet shows and gently guided and inspired her young patrons. An active member and officer of the Montana Library Association, Smith worked with the library's board of trustees to incorporate countywide library services in 1957. Between 1959 and 1962, Smith engaged with the Montana State Library Commission to establish Miles City as the headquarters of the Sagebrush Federation of Libraries, which offered cooperative services—bookmobiles, expanded collections, and training—among five eastern Montana counties.

The library staff's capacity to serve outpaced the building's physical capacity by 1965. That year, a city-county bond matched a $61,116 Library Services and Construction Act grant to remodel the space, replace the windows, and build an addition. Though the modern one-story addition obscured the original façade, it nearly doubled the library's square footage. The new space provided accessibility, community space, and more room for the collection, which had tripled over the course of the decade. Smith worked with assistant librarian Muriel Dahlin Cooksey to curate the Montana Room, a special collection associated with the state's early history, and to effectively manage the Sagebrush Federation's multicounty consortium. Cooksey became head librarian upon Smith's retirement. Though wholeheartedly dedicated to the library, Cooksey resisted computerization, and she "happily retired" as the digital age progressed during the 1980s.

Since that time, the library has embraced technology by offering Internet access, technology classes, online databases, and digitized collections. Encased within its modern frame and within its remodeled interior, the Miles City Carnegie library's physical character may have changed, but its heart and mission remain the same: "to provide free access to information, educational and recreational materials, and lifelong learning opportunities."

▲ Laura Manderscheid Brown Zook, who arrived in newly founded Miles City by steamboat when she was ten, served as the Miles City librarian from 1903 to 1941. IMAGE COURTESY MONTANA HISTORICAL SOCIETY PAC 97-6-2.

▲ The 1965 addition constructed across the front and side elevations provided extra square footage and an accessible entry, but obscured most of Haire's original design.

▲ The children's section of the Miles City Public Library remains a popular destination for Custer County families.

▲ Glimpses of the Miles City Carnegie library's former grandeur are still found in the large historic reading room on the upper floor.

"PUBLIC LIBRARY" GREAT FALLS MONT.

GREAT FALLS

Located within a broad, sweeping curve of the Missouri River, the city of Great Falls owes its situation to businessman Paris Gibson and, like many other Montana cities, to railroad magnate James Hill. Where others saw the five waterfalls of the Missouri as an obstacle to be avoided or a scenic tourist attraction, the two men recognized the area's potential for providing hydroelectric power and coal resources as Hill planned his transcontinental route across the Montana Territory. Platted in 1883, the city boasted two hundred residents the following year and six times as many people by 1887. It continued to grow exponentially through the subsequent decades.

As early as 1886, Great Falls residents established a literary society and proposed the idea of a town library association, declaring that "special police will have to be appointed to keep back the eager throng who will rush to join." Talk of the Young Men's Christian Association opening a library and reading room appeared in the *Great Falls Tribune* in late 1887. Mrs. F. A. Reynolds outlined the need for a deterrent to drunkenness in May 1888: "What is my idea? Why, open a reading room and library!"

Valeria Goodenow Gibson, Paris Gibson's wife, took great interest in the library beginning in spring 1889, after several newspaper articles called out the need. The Valeria Library and Art Association opened a public reading room and circulating library in a commercial block on January 20, 1890, collecting fees for its use. Librarian Robert Williams oversaw the eight-hundred-volume collection as plans progressed to construct a dedicated building. The delightful one-story brick Valeria Library opened in March 1891. But within a year, the library association had fallen into debt and offered its assets to

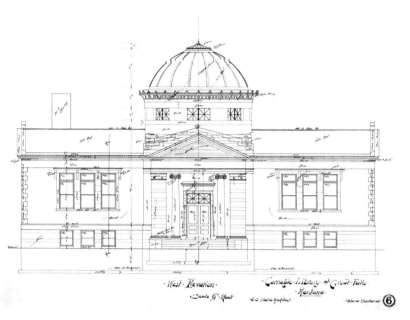

▲ Charles S. Haire's design for the Great Falls Public Library was ambitious, featuring a central dome and a stately columned entrance, reflecting the optimism and prosperity of the city and its promoters. It was the largest Carnegie library built in Montana and the most expensive ($31,700).
IMAGE COURTESY MSU-BOZEMAN 2040-F306-006

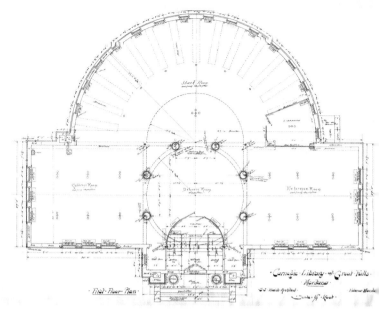

▲ Haire's floor plan provided direction on how the interior library spaces were used, including a retrieval desk for the closed stack room that filled the building's semicircular wing. The children's room occupied space in the basement, accessed by a side door.
IMAGE COURTESY MSU-BOZEMAN 2040-F306-003

the city. In April 1892, Great Falls' citizenry voted overwhelmingly in favor of accepting the deal, as well as to support the library with a half-mill levy that provided at least $3,000 annually. The building reopened as the free public library on May 11, 1892.

By 1900 the library was bursting at the seams with more than five thousand volumes. The city built an addition in 1901, but at the same time the Great Falls Business Men's Association wrote to Carnegie extolling the virtues of the city, reporting on the library's statistics, and asking for $50,000 for an entirely new building.

Carnegie's personal secretary, James Bertram, offered $30,000 on June 21, 1901, and the city put out a call for bids for the new building. Amid controversy, the city council chose Charles S. Haire's submission for a

monumental Renaissance Revival design embellished with Ionic columns, a domed rotunda, and a semicircular rear extension. Butte firm Goddard and Smith landed the contract. Nearly a year later, the library still wasn't complete. The *Great Falls Tribune* reported that "nobody so far has been found who will assume any responsibility for the botched job, but whether it's the architect, the contractors or someone else, the public has a right to know something about it." The paper changed its tune upon the building's opening on October 15, 1903: "The new building . . . is a structure of which the trustees are proud. Its interior arrangement is admirable, following that of the best libraries in the land. . . . The building is splendidly lighted. The ceilings are high, the finish seems excellent, and the arrangement appears most convenient."

▲ This view of the Great Falls Carnegie library includes the older Valeria Library building at the far left (north). The city demolished the Valeria building in 1961 and the Carnegie library in 1965. A modern $1.2 million public library opened on the same site in 1967.

The new library offered more than six thousand volumes, overseen by professional librarian Jennie M. Conner. Conner, who had been appointed librarian in 1902, introduced improved cataloging and a patron-friendly open shelf system that allowed the public to physically browse the collection. At the library board's bidding, Conner wrote to Carnegie in January 1906 and received an additional $1,700 to cover the original construction debt.

The population and the commensurate demand for services grew substantially over the next four years. By 1910, the need to convert some of the lower level space into a children's reading room became apparent. At the risk of annoying Mr. Carnegie, the library board again wrote to ask for more money, which Carnegie denied. Instead, the city's populace raised the funds to make the children's room a reality.

When Conner's tenure as librarian ended in 1913, the board appointed Louise M. Fernald in her place. Fernald proved to be a worthy successor for the next three decades, promoting outreach, working with the state library association and the American Library Association, and reclaiming the old Valeria building for cataloging space and storage. Together with children's librarian Josephine Trigg, Fernald witnessed a great increase in patronage at the height of the Great Depression, when the library offered a refuge to the unemployed. Both librarians retired in June 1945, after a combined sixty-eight years of service.

Margaret Fulmer began her service as city librarian in 1945. She left to take a faculty position at the University of Minnesota in September 1952, but upon her resignation she warned that the Carnegie Building and Valeria Building Annex provided insufficient space for the collection. Lucille H. Simpson replaced Fulmer. During her year-long stay, the city remodeled the building to improve energy efficiency and systems but left the interior "cramped and dark." Great Falls native Alma Smith Jacobs, who had worked as a catalog librarian there since 1946, was appointed librarian in 1954.

Jacobs's appointment marked a turning point. In addition to her social and political activism, she strove to make the library a place to enable young people and adults to advance themselves, often stating that "the public library is the poor man's university." Her work earned her Woman of the Year honors from the Great Falls Business and Professional Women's Club in 1957, the same year she was elected president of the Pacific Northwest Library Association. She agitated for a new, modern library building for nearly a decade; after two failed levy votes, her efforts succeeded in 1965. The bond covered $900,000, and a Library Services and Construction Act grant paid for the balance of the $1.2 million cost. The city decided to raze the Carnegie library to make way for the new building. The last patron was served in the well-loved and well-used Carnegie on September 4, 1965.

For the new library, the firm of McIver and Hess Architects created a design in a New Formalist style—a modern interpretation of classical elements. The building comprised three stories plus a full basement, with rooms designated for special collections, audiovisual equipment, meeting space, children's programming, storage, and offices. Dedicated on November 12, 1967, the new library was hailed as "beautiful and functional . . . one of the most impressive buildings in the city."

Over the next fifty years, the library expanded its services beyond Great Falls' residents by providing mobile services to those outside the city and by supporting independent community libraries in Belt and Cascade. Though the city's population plateaued after 1970, services, innovation, and the building itself continued to be improved. A renovation in 1989 remediated asbestos, installed new carpet, and reconfigured some of the interior spaces, including enlarging the children's room. The 1990s witnessed a revolution in technology, with the first dial-up Internet service introduced in 1995. Today, patrons use the spaces for research, entertainment, conferences, and, of course, reading. The Great Falls Public Library stands as a vital part of the city's cultural legacy.

The Interior of the Carnegie Library,
Great Falls, Montana.

Montana Library Association Ninth annual meeting Great Falls Nov. 22-24, 1915 Put this on your desk and plan to attend

Miss Josephine Haley Public Library Helena Montana

▲ The front and back of this postcard depicts the Great Falls Carnegie library's interior columns, domed ceiling, and central circulation desk in 1915. The penmanship on the back side shows the "library hand" penmanship style of then-librarian Louise Fernald. IMAGE COURTESY MONTANA HISTORICAL SOCIETY, 947-908

BOZEMAN

THE GALLATIN VALLEY BECKONED TRIBAL NATIONS for millennia, and non-Indian trappers filtered into the area by the early nineteenth century. Miners traveled through during the 1860s, soon followed by farmers and town builders. In 1863, Georgia-born adventurer and gold seeker John Bozeman and his guide, John M. Jacobs, followed Indian trails and trappers' traces to blaze a shortcut to Montana's goldfields. Though in service for only two years, the Bozeman Trail carried thousands of emigrants. In 1864 Bozeman, along with Daniel Rouse and William Beall, founded the city of Bozeman, situated to "swallow up all the tenderfeet" as they arrived from the East.

Many of the city's early residents recognized the need for social enrichment, including a library. In 1872, the new Gallatin County Bar Association founded a Young Men's Association (YMA), following a national model of subscription libraries, and opened their own meeting hall and reading rooms. The local newspaper lauded the endeavor: "a public library is a necessity. . . . It will give our boys and young men some place besides the saloon and gambling house to spend their evenings and leisure hours." Women could access the library during afternoon hours a few days a week, while the gentlemen were permitted only in the evening on Thursdays and Saturdays. Unfortunately, the Panic of 1873 and the subsequent economic depression took its toll on Bozeman and its institutions, and the YMA disbanded in December 1875. The library's collection fell into disuse and eventually was moved to the public school.

In 1884, the YMA's library association trustees transferred its funds and inventory to the Young Men's Christian Association (YMCA). Like its predecessor, the YMCA offered subscription access to its library. Local women supported the venture by serving as part-time librarians and volunteers. Again, the library was seen

▲ Charles Haire's 1903 plans for the Bozeman Carnegie library resembled his design for his earlier Miles City Carnegie library. Bozeman's stately brick building featured a Greek-cross floor plan—a tall central hall flanked on either side by single-story reading rooms—as well as a rear semicircular collections area and a pedimented front entry.
IMAGE COURTESY MSU-BOZEMAN 0863-F330-009

▲ Similar to his design for the Great Falls Carnegie library, though more modest in scale, Haire chose a half-octagon footprint for the collections area at the rear of the Bozeman Carnegie library.

at least partly as a way of keeping males out of trouble: in 1886, the newspaper observed, "This philanthropic enterprise deserves the hearty support of every citizen interested in the good morals of our boys and young men." However, public efforts could not pull the library out of a "slough of despond," and it closed in October 1888. A fire engulfed the collection just six months later. The remnants, about 250 volumes, were relocated to a donated space while a civic-minded few rallied to keep the library accessible. They succeeded in 1891, when the city instituted a half-mill library levy. This investment allowed it to flourish for the first time, and the collection expanded to nearly 5,300 volumes by 1900.

A victim of its own success, the massive collection began to overtake its rooms in City Hall. Librarian Bell Chrisman made inquiries about a new building and, together with the city library committee's chair, J. M. Lindley, and City Clerk T. M. Pierce, applied to Carnegie for funds on October 30, 1901. Carnegie's secretary, James Bertram, responded encouragingly, asking for more details and clarifications. Because Bozeman already had a tax-supported library in place, the application process went smoothly. On March 14, 1902, Bertram promised Bozeman $15,000 for a building, provided the city increase its levy and obtain a proper building lot. In April 1902, the city increased the library levy to one mill, allowing for approximately $2,000 per year to be dedicated to library expenses.

Chrisman and her compatriots, including the Woman's Christian Temperance Union, lobbied the city to locate the library in accordance with the City Beautiful movement's mantra that beauty could encourage order and propriety. They sought to counteract squalid conditions and nefarious behaviors by introducing cultural institutions to less prosperous areas. The corner of Mendenhall and Bozeman, notorious for its "female boarding" establishments, was a prime location. Like the YMA and YMCA before them, Chrisman and her associates believed that the library's presence would entice young men to choose enlightenment over alternative forms of recreation.

Architect Charles S. Haire offered extensive library design experience—this would be his fourth Carnegie library commission in Montana in two years. For Bozeman, he envisioned an elaborate edifice, with a modified Greek-cross footprint, pedimented entry, columns, and quoining, in keeping with City Beautiful's espousal of classically inspired architecture. In the interior, the tower's clerestory—a series of windows around the tower base—illuminated the central lobby, while tall windows delivered natural light to the reading rooms and stacks in the wings. The daylight basement provided additional meeting and storage space. The city embraced Haire's design, and construction commenced within a year. A dedication ceremony on January 19, 1904, included an open house in the new building.

Fifteen years later, librarian Geneva Cook wrote to the Carnegie Corporation of New York about possible funding for a county library. Wishing "to take advantage of the [recently passed] Montana County Library Law," both the city and county officials were "anxious to establish a library"

Carnegie Library, Bozeman, Mont.

▲ Charles Haire designed Montana's first four Carnegie libraries. His elegant, classically inspired building for Bozeman featured smooth brick exterior walls upon a rough-cut stone daylight basement.
IMAGE COURTESY MONTANA HISTORICAL SOCIETY, PC-OOI BOZE 2596

but required financial aid to do so. Unfortunately for the county, by spring 1919, the Carnegie Corporation had ceased its library building program. The Bozeman Public Library remained a city institution and served the public from its Carnegie-funded building for eighty years. It provided not only reading materials and reference services but also community meeting spaces and public programs.

By 1979, the building's capacity to accommodate a growing population, additional programming, computer technology, and digital services proved challenging. The city's residents voted to have a new library constructed a few blocks away. Volunteers carried the collections to the new library on July 14, 1981. City offices took over the Carnegie building, but accessibility issues and deferred maintenance led the city to consider demolition

▲ Home to a law firm today, the Bozeman Carnegie library retains its graceful lines and symmetry.

in the mid-1990s. Fortunately, local historic preservation supporters rallied to save it. Attorneys Mike Cok and Mike Wheat purchased the old library and undertook an extensive, sensitive rehabilitation.

But the spacious 1981 library, set on a creek-side parcel, also became cramped as collections, programming, and technology expanded over the next two decades. In a familiar pattern, city offices took over the building when a new library opened in November 2006. Reminiscent of the Carnegie library, the new space was constructed in a prominent location, with an imposing yet welcoming edifice. Nearly ten times as large as Haire's Neoclassical Revival design of 1904, the thoroughly modern building

accommodates Bozeman's rapidly expanding population with high-tech services and equipment while retaining a sense of warmth and dedication to public service.

While a library had served the city since 1872, Bozeman's Carnegie library constituted the first stand-alone library building in the city when it was completed in 1904. Carnegie's gift established the new library as a definitive cultural institution. Saved from demolition ninety years after its construction, the Bozeman Carnegie library building continues to contribute to the city's architectural landscape and to remind the public of the community's long-standing commitment to cultural and educational enrichment.

▲ Although no longer a library, the modern office reception area intentionally mimics the original librarians' desk and circulation space.

▲ A portrait of Andrew Carnegie still hangs proudly in the tall entry hall. Artist F. Luis Mora painted this popular image of Carnegie, widely reproduced for Carnegie libraries across the country.

KALISPELL

RELATIVELY FEW NON-INDIAN SETTLERS LIVED IN the Upper Flathead Valley area until the 1880s, when the Northern Pacific Railway completed its railroad line to Ravalli and water travel across Flathead Lake became well established. In 1891, the Great Northern Railways' impending arrival prompted a businessman and banker named Charles Conrad to found the city of Kalispell near the confluence of the Stillwater, Whitefish, and Flathead Rivers. Bolstered by the lumber and milling industries, the young community embraced its role as a railroad division point and commercial center.

With stability came families, the introduction of civic and social institutions, and of course, the need for libraries. The Knights of Pythias Hall housed the first public reading room in 1892, and the Nineteenth Century Club, a women's organization that included Charles Conrad's wife, Alicia Conrad, established the Ladies Library Association and the town's first circulating library in 1894. They loaned out their collection of donated books from various locations until the local women's club opened the six-hundred-volume Kalispell Public Library on December 20, 1897.

The women's club "bore the burden of expense" for running the library until 1900, when Kalispell voted in favor of a tax-supported free city public library. The city hired Florence Madison, who had a "thorough knowledge of the name and number of every volume," as the city librarian. Wishing for a "very fine" library building, the local newspaper pressured the library board to take advantage of Andrew Carnegie's "determination not to die rich" and request a library construction grant. J. W. Conner of the city's Board of Trade and J. H. Edwards of Conrad National Bank wrote separately to Carnegie in November 1901, conveying not only Kalispell's rosy economic situation and prospects

▲ Designed by architect George Shanley, the Kalispell Carnegie library cost just under $10,000 to build in 1904. The Second Renaissance Revival style featured a grand octagonal dome, bracketed eaves, carved sandstone trim, and pilastered bay windows.
IMAGE COURTESY MONTANA HISTORICAL SOCIETY, PL001 KALI-BLDGS

▲ Although some of Shanley's original decorative elements were scaled back to reduce costs, numerous ornamentations grace the building's exterior.

but also brief histories of the city's library. James Bertram responded on behalf of Carnegie with a $10,000 offer.

The day after Edwards received Bertram's letter, the city passed a resolution accepting the gift and its conditions. Deciding upon and acquiring the building site proved more time-consuming. Deeming them "as good as could be procured without paying an exorbitant price," the city purchased two lots on the southwest corner of Third Street East and Second Avenue East in May 1902. With Bertram's approval, the newly formed library building committee worked with the city to select the architect and develop plans over the next few months.

A regional architectural firm, Gibson and Shanley, offered the winning design. As drawn by architect George Shanley, the building was to measure fifty-six by sixty feet,

with the main story set upon a daylight basement, and it would feature a large central dome. When the first round of construction bids came in above the $10,000 limit, Edwards wrote Carnegie to ask for more money. Bertram declined, so the library board worked with Shanley to scale back the design. Shanley's revisions, which called for a nearly square building with a pyramidal roof and a domed, octagonal corner entry, was accepted in January 1903.

The architect's father, contractor Bernard Shanley, won the construction bid and soon got to work. Completed in November 1903 for a cost of $9,860, the building "look[ed] every inch a library." The Renaissance Revival design included deep, bracketed eaves above a pillared entry. The main story of Menominee red brick with carved blue-sandstone trim distinguished the building

▲ Shanley created a rectangular, one-story library of imported Menominee red brick above a rough sandstone basement. The bracketed eaves beneath the roof line stand out in this side and rear view.

further. Shallow hipped extensions at the north and east elevations, set off by sandstone-capped pilasters, provided additional visual interest and depth. Though somewhat grand, Shanley's design was also practical, allowing librarians at the central circulation desk to see into the interior's reading rooms, stacks, and reference areas.

Shanley senior completed major construction in November 1903, and a dedication reception took place on January 12, 1904. The building was ready for patronage two weeks later, and the city added furnishings and decorations by February 1904. Florence Madison stayed on as librarian through the transition to the new building;

librarian and author Katherine Berry Judson replaced her in 1905. In 1907, a strained budget, high patronage, and inefficient spaces prompted the library board and newly appointed librarian Janet Nunn to ask Carnegie for $1,500 to finish the basement rooms and furnish the children's room. That request was not granted, and the board wrote Carnegie again in 1910 asking for up to $6,000 for an addition. Though the city's population had nearly doubled since 1900, Bertram rejected that request as well.

Over the next decade, library staff advertised new books and library hours in the newspaper and made considerable efforts to engage young readers: "The

▲ Shanley envisioned a warm and inviting foyer beneath the library's octagonal dome. Today, that floor plan remains intact and the foyer provides access to the reception desk and spacious galleries, formerly collections and reading spaces.

Carnegie library of Kalispell has long been one of the city's greatest prides. The building has always been well taken care of; the grounds have always been a delight to passers-by; the best of literature has been available and competent and courteous librarians have attended to the wants of the patrons. . . . This library is chiefly for the benefit of the boys and girls of this community. It is THEIR library."

By 1930, the library housed approximately thirteen thousand volumes, and the need for additional space continued to be an issue over the subsequent decades. Though Flathead County established its own separate library in the early 1940s, Kalispell residents patronized the library heavily through the 1950s, and the city's collection continued to grow. The long campaign to finish and utilize the basement as a children's room finally came to fruition in 1953. Thanks to a national Library Services Act grant, the library also reclaimed its coal- and wood-storage rooms for an activity space in 1957.

While the improvements were welcome, by the late 1960s, the library had run out of space to expand. The city and county began discussions about consolidating into a single space. The plan to combine the two libraries included remodeling the former post office building across the street from the Carnegie library. Local architects William C. Bierrum Associates converted the space. The Flathead County library budgeted $10,000, Kalispell instituted a one-time-only three-mill levy, and the state provided $75,000 in matching funds to pay for the project. The converted historic building more than doubled the libraries' previous spaces. Meanwhile, the Flathead Valley Art Association sought to establish a Flathead Valley art center, and the Kalispell Carnegie library appeared a perfect fit: "Central location, distinctive character, and adaptability make the Carnegie Library building an ideal site for the art center." Named the Hockaday Center for the Arts, after local artist Hugh Hockaday, the converted Carnegie library opened on February 10, 1969.

The Flathead County Library continues to provide regional services from the old post office building. Over the past fifty years, that institution has modernized and expanded its reach to keep pace with the technological needs of its patrons. At the same time, the Hockaday Center's focus has shifted to museum activities, and the building was renamed the Hockaday Museum of Art in 1998, establishing itself as a premier center for art in the area. Melding its modern mission with its respect for the past, the Hockaday continues to celebrate and preserve the precious features of its historic building.

▲ The intricately carved oak stairwell invites patrons to a large basement area.

MISSOULA

Gertrude Buckhous was born on her family's farm south of Missoula in 1881. A book lover from a young age, she pursued her studies at the University of Montana and graduated in 1900—one of seven students in her class. After studying library science in the Midwest, she returned to her hometown and alma mater in 1902, just as the city was asking Andrew Carnegie for a library building. As the newly hired librarian at University of Montana (named Montana State University from 1913 to 1965), Buckhous teamed with the local effort, and thus began her nearly thirty-year career supporting libraries statewide.

In 1882, just a year after Buckhous' birth, local ladies formed a reading group. A Chautauqua Circle followed in 1885, and then a subscription library in 1890. By 1894, the city boasted a library of five hundred volumes: "200 volumes of Congressional Records and reports and 300 volumes of history, fiction, etc., . . . a very good collection to start with." That year, the city residents voted in favor of a half-mill levy to support a public library; five years later, the levy increased to one mill. Operated out of rented rooms on the third story of a downtown business block, the collection grew steadily, approaching five thousand volumes by 1902.

In January 1903, the local women's club wrote to Andrew Carnegie to convey Missoula's "crying need" for a dedicated library building. Not only was the location cramped and inconvenient, but the rented building's potential sale jeopardized the library's future. Over the previous year, the library board and Mayor Albert Miles Stevens had written to Carnegie also, and Carnegie's secretary, James Bertram, gave them notice of a $12,500 gift on January 13, 1903. Stevens assured Bertram that Missoula's new library would "redound to the greater glory of the giver and the moral and mental advancement of the present and future members of this community."

▲ A. J. Gibson's rectangular library consisted of a main story with a monumental entry, wide staircase, and Doric columns. Its Neoclassical Revival style included architectural elements that became hallmarks of the Carnegie Classic design. IMAGE COURTESY MONTANA HISTORICAL SOCIETY, 949-502

▲ Exterior adornments on the Missoula Carnegie library included an elegant, monumental front entry and contrasting brick details around the windows.

Missoula residents began a spirited discussion regarding the library site. Many living in the relatively affluent neighborhoods south of the river wished the library be built there, and they offered to sweeten the deal via donated lots from Margaret Daly, widow of the wealthy Copper King, Marcus Daly. Mrs. Daly offered an additional $5,000 to improve the building's quality and appearance. North and west side residents protested, arguing that the library was intended "for rich and poor alike [and] . . . should be placed where it would do the most good." A west sider proposed a location on his side of town, "if only for the moral effect it would have on us ignoramuses." In March, the city council settled on two large, publicly owned lots north of the river, at the southwest corner of Pattee and Pine Streets, just east of downtown. The following month's call for architectural bids yielded three contenders: J. F. Everett of Butte, Haire and Fennell of Helena, and Missoula's A. J. Gibson, who submitted a bid with another local architect, John H. Kennedy. Though Charles Haire had experience designing libraries in Billings, Dillon, Miles City, and Great Falls, Gibson and Kennedy won out.

Gibson took the lead on the project. While he had no specific library design experience, Gibson did boast a number of monumental public buildings in his portfolio, including the University of Montana campus. His partiality toward the Neoclassical Revival style rang true in his first library offering, a "universally praised" and "exemplary" design. Gibson's rectangular building featured a main story atop a daylight basement, a centered pedimented entry, and a dentiled metal cornice around the base of the hipped roof; in subsequent decades these features coincidentally became hallmarks of Carnegie Classic design. Light brick highlighted the entry, basement level, and window openings, while orange-red brick constituted the main story's exterior walls. Doric columns flanked the primary entrance and appeared in pairs on the interior as well, defining the central circulation space apart from the reading room and stacks wings to either side. Richly appointed wood trims, moldings, and mantels appeared throughout and added warmth and approachability to the formal symmetry and proportions.

When it opened to "a long line" of patrons on September 17, 1904, the "elegant" building was lauded by the *Missoulian* as "one of the best in the entire state." Newly hired librarian Grace Stoddard oversaw the transition to the new building and introduced new systems as well, including collection indexes and catalogs. Stoddard, who was professionally educated, took great interest in library best practices and service. A founding member of the Montana State Library Association in 1906, she worked closely with university librarian Gertrude Buckhous to bolster the profession and, later, to foster the creation of county libraries statewide.

Missoula's population nearly tripled between 1900 and 1910. In 1911, Stoddard and the president of the library association, J. H. T. Ryman, reported to Carnegie a substantial increase in Missoula's collection and patronage. As a result, the library required more space. Architect Ole Bakke, Gibson's protégé, offered a solution via a second-story addition. After extensive negotiations, Bertram agreed, and the Carnegie Corporation increased its gift by $9,000. Bakke's Craftsman-style-inspired stucco-clad addition introduced ganged windows and quoining beneath a deep, unadorned boxed eave, without obscuring the essence of Gibson's design.

Completed in 1913, the addition allowed for a dedicated children's room, more stacks, and a glassed-off

▲ The children's area of the Missoula Carnegie library was used often by the growing community. Note the very full bookshelves behind this ca. 1950 story hour crowd. IMAGE COURTESY MONTANA HISTORICAL SOCIETY, PAC 2002-3 B2

▲ In 2007 the Missoula Art Museum completed an addition, using a glass transitional hyphen to link the new structure to the original Carnegie library.

▲ The transitional structure between the original and new museum spaces offers excellent views of the external walls of Gibson's first floor and Bakke's second story library.

periodicals division. Stoddard and Buckhous championed the idea of countywide library services and used Missoula's city library to lead by example. They enjoyed "conspicuous success" with their extension programs, which brought the city's collections to surrounding locales. Their efforts included advocacy for the state's County Library Law, which was passed in 1915 and allowed counties to levy up to one mill for library services. The following year, Stoddard ushered to success the petition to establish Missoula's designation for a county library, which also operated out of the Carnegie building. After fourteen years of "unselfish, intelligent, and enthusiastic service," Stoddard resigned and moved out of state to care for her father.

The library board hired Elizabeth Powell to replace her as the city's librarian and named Ruth Worden county librarian. Worden remained county librarian until 1927, when Powell added those duties to her own, until her

resignation in 1934. Over her sixteen years of service, the collection more than doubled in size, and circulation tripled, in part because of innovative programs like children's story hours and a railcar library that delivered volumes to logging districts. Missoula's tradition of retaining dedicated long-term librarians continued with Nina Ford (1934 to 1947) and Evelyn Swant (1947 to 1970).

The national Library Services Act of 1956 facilitated the establishment of the Five Valleys Federation of Libraries in 1957, a cooperative service whereby member libraries participated in collective development and used a centralized processing center. These improvements tested the Carnegie library's capacity. Swant publicly advocated for a new building, reporting in 1967 that "additional space was desperately needed if the library were to continue to serve the public in its current manner," and by 1969 the search for a new building site was in full

▲ Interior paired Doric columns originally framed the library's circulation area and were retained during modern renovations. Other original features were removed, including the rich wood trim, moldings, and mantels.

swing. Swant retired before Missoula passed an $850,000 bond for a new library on June 6, 1972. Librarian William H. Snyder oversaw the transition when the new building on Main Street opened on April 1, 1974.

Also in 1974, the city signed a lease with the Missoula Arts Council and allotted $25,000 to rehabilitate the Carnegie building for use as a museum. The county joined in by supporting the Missoula Art Museum's operations with a mill levy. With few physical changes to the building, the museum flourished, so much so that the institution began planning another major renovation and expansion in the early 2000s. A modern addition now occupies the south side of the property and connects to the original building via a metal and glass hyphen that serves as the entrance. Completed in 2007, the multimillion-dollar addition and rehabilitation design kept the east and south elevations of the Carnegie exterior intact but modified the

second-story windows at the rear (west) wall and completely obscured the south side of the original building. The renovation removed the interior's original features and finishes—pairs of columns that defined the library's central lobby are all that remain. This modern museum enjoys a high level of public and private support, and recent plans promise to reintroduce historic elements, including bringing the original entry back into use.

Meanwhile, the Missoula City-County Library's board supported a successful $30 million bond issue for a new library that passed in 2016. Construction on the four-story building, designed by A&E Architects, began in 2018 and will provide 121,000 square feet of space for library services, technological expansion, video production, and nonprofit organizations. Missoulians have once again proved that their capacity to rally behind their library has only increased over its 140-year history.

LIVINGSTON

IN NOVEMBER 1900, THE MEMBERS OF THE YELLOW-stone Club of Livingston—founded by a group of about twenty women in 1892—rallied for a free public library in their city. They aroused a "lively interest," and within four months they had gathered donations sufficient to ask the city council for space. The library was housed in a room within the city hall and firehouse building on Callender Street, and the women took turns providing access about four hours a week. The ladies also successfully canvased their fellow citizens to obtain a "numerously signed petition" to institute a one-mill levy supporting the endeavor.

Formally organized with a board of trustees in May 1902, the library proved popular, but the designated space did not. Intent to provide "better accommodations for patrons than could be had in city hall," including a reading room, the city authorized renting space in a "centrally and conveniently located" downtown commercial building

for $30 a month. The city furnished the three rooms, increased the number of volumes available to patrons, and employed a librarian. Newspapers as far away as Butte announced the news: "The Livingston Public Library has been removed to spacious quarters on Callender Street. An attractive room has been opened and extra effort shall be put forth by those in charge to conduct an up-to-date reading room. The rooms have been tastefully arranged by a committee of ladies and no pain has been spared to give the public first-class service."

While the city officials and Yellowstone Club members made considerable efforts to provide a welcoming space, they did not intend the accommodations to be permanent; a dedicated building would be ideal. In February 1902, City Clerk M. R. Wilson wrote to Andrew Carnegie on the city's behalf, having "noticed from time to time that certain cities and towns," including several in Montana,

▲ Completed in 1904, Charles E. Bell's brick and stone Carnegie library for Livingston cost $9,750. The monumental entrance with gold lettering reflected the community's lofty goals. IMAGE COURTESY MONTANA HISTORICAL SOCIETY, PAC 2013-50 LIVI-BLDGS.

received "liberal donations for public libraries." Hearing no reply, Wilson wrote again in February and one more time in May. Carnegie's secretary, James Bertram, offered little apology when he responded in January 1903: "Yours of May 16th just taken up. Please give some particulars of the Library, its work and accommodation. Being a small community, the quarters in City Hall might be sufficient."

Though hardly an encouraging response, the city found the reply "highly satisfactory" and was quite confident that "when the facts are placed before Mr. Carnegie the donation for a library will be forthcoming." Mayor Charles Garnier quickly and enthusiastically offered the history of the library and its statistics, as well as a glowing portrait of the city. He also relayed that the need for a building was "very keenly felt," especially to accommodate the "large number of unmarried men who desire good books" and the many children who availed themselves of the "features that a library furnishes." Bertram sent the good news in March that Carnegie would gift the city $10,000. The local newspaper claimed that the offer met "with the approval of every citizen of this city."

The city officials and library board got down to business and completed the transactions and resolutions required. They chose lots that faced Callender Street, just a block from the new railroad depot, and close to the other civic buildings in town, but on the edge of the commercial area's interface with residential development. Though some community members marveled at the library board's "splendid inactivity," the officials had arrangements in place to call for architectural bids by early summer 1903. Charles E. Bell, a Helena-based architect who had recently completed both the Montana State Capitol (with his partner John Kent) and Livingston's West Side School, narrowly won the bid with his "handsome, commodious and convenient" interpretation of Neoclassical Revival design. When the construction bids came in, the library board abandoned their hopes for an all-stone building—the cost was prohibitive—and reverted to Bell's original brick-and-stone suggestion. Local builder H. J. Wolcott received the construction contract for $9,750.

Over the course of the next year, the modified cross-shaped edifice took shape on a grassy, raised corner lot. The daylight basement's flared, tall, rough-faced Columbus sandstone blocks offered weight and grounded the tan Dickinson-brick upper story. Stone steps climbed up to Bell's monumental projecting entry. A second flight progressed through an arched recess to the paired oak doors. Engaged fluted columns simulated a colonnade supporting the dentiled cornice and paneled parapet wall. The building's window openings rose to nearly the main story's full height. In the interior, a sixteen-foot-high main story featured wood-trim finishes and plasterwork at the central delivery desk, children's library, stacks area, and reference room.

In preparation for the move, Livingston's librarian Eleanor Hamilton attended classes at the University of Minnesota's library school during the summer of 1904. The training allowed her to catalog and oversee the collection's transfer to the new building that September and October. Hamilton rewarded the Yellowstone Club's

▲ Children's programming has always been an important mission for the Livingston library. Here, a large group of local children show off their newly built birdhouses in front of their Carnegie library, ca. 1920. Original print photographed by Tom Ferris. IMAGE COURTESY PARK COUNTY LIBRARY.

▲ The Livingston Carnegie library's original daylight basement today offers plenty of space for children's programming and collections.

▲ Today the large rectangular windows of Bell's original design are still accentuated by the dentiled cornice above.

commitment to the library by offering the members a private tour on October 24, one day before the general public opening. The club members "expressed unqualified approval" and subsequently held their weekly meetings in the assembly room. Livingston patrons made full use of the well-appointed facility, which was open daily, and held a gala grand opening ceremony the following spring.

Though often underfunded, the Livingston library saw a steady increase in circulation and patronage through the 1910s. The library served not only as an information hub but also as a community space, often doubling as a classroom or exhibition hall. By 1917, cramped

storage and reading room areas necessitated an "extensive repair and improvement project." Livingston residents again voted their support for the library in 1920 by doubling the levy to two mills. Traveling libraries and nonresidential borrowing policies offered service over an extensive area, and the idea of establishing a Park County library, as well as the need for renovations, additional funding, and more space, remained constant themes for decades.

A major renovation during the early 1950s helped make the interior more efficient, but funding for more space did not materialize until the 1970s. In 1976, the library formally transitioned to a city-county entity. A new Friends of the Library group successfully campaigned for $209,000 in city and county contributions, and the resulting addition in 1978 extended the building's north wing and added street-level access with a new entrance facing Third Street. Twenty years later, and led by the Friends of the Library, the community again rallied for another addition. Beginning with reintroducing historically accurate windows and repairing the original building, the new campaign brought in an exceptional number of contributions, and the modern space opened in 2005. Architecturally distinct, the $1.3 million two-story expansion doubled the library's original footprint.

As the Livingston-Park County Public Library enters its second century, the building testifies to the community's ongoing commitment to respecting its rich past while embracing the future. The Yellowstone Club continues to meet in the library, as it has since its opening days, and the dedicated library staff carries on the tradition of outstanding, courteous assistance. Meanwhile, updated technology and new programming allow for innovation within this long-standing, beloved community institution.

▲ In 1978 and again in 2005, the Livingston library expanded toward the rear of the lot, retaining the original look and feel at the front but offering much-needed additional space for collections and services to the rear.

▲ Bell's original design created impressive interiors featuring sixteen-foot-high ceilings and large open spaces. Today the Livingston-Park County Public Library still offers generous stacks and reading areas beneath skylighted ceilings.

LEWISTOWN

In January 1897, the editors of the *Fergus County Argus* pitched their readers on the need for a library. With $35 remaining in a fund from a previous unsuccessful effort, all that was needed, they explained, was books, space, and someone to run it—perhaps "some lady, whose time would permit, might be glad to assume duties."

The next month, Lewistown resident Mary Hanson took up the call, offering space in her millinery store and volunteering her time and organizational skills. A library committee traveled door to door collecting books and asking for subscriptions, resulting in a nascent collection of 269 books and a fund totaling $91.50. While some residents considered a subscription library preferable, the majority voted to keep the library "absolutely free to all . . . who will abide by the rules of society." Hanson oversaw the collection's growth by several hundred volumes and served as the city's volunteer librarian for two years, when she and her family moved away.

The Lewistown library's next iteration, in 1899, offered circulation of more than seven hundred volumes from the Fergus County Superintendent of Schools office but lacked a reading room. In that cramped space, Elizabeth Peebles performed the duties of both superintendent and librarian for two years. Early in 1901, the Lewistown City Council voted to pursue establishing an official city library, "where young and old, rich and poor alike may have free access to the best literature." The council unanimously passed Ordinance 30, allowing for a one-mill levy to support library services, in April. The collection moved to the Hawthorne School, and Mary A. Sloan became the city's first paid librarian, at a salary of $10 per month.

The partitioned space off the school hallway soon proved inadequate, and in 1902 library board chairman Frank Smith, board members, and prominent citizens began writing to Andrew Carnegie to ask for a building

Carnegie Library, Lewistown, Mont.

▲ Completed in 1905 for $14,000, the Lewistown Carnegie library sits on a grassy hill at the west end of Main Street. Jeff Tubb's Neoclassical Revival design paired sandstone columns with a central arched doorway below a pedimented roof. IMAGE COURTESY MONTANA HISTORICAL SOCIETY, 949-004

▲ Built by local Croatian stonemasons, the Lewistown Carnegie library boasted carved stone brackets under the eaves and handcrafted terracotta ornamentation above smooth- and rough-cut sandstone blocks. IMAGE COURTESY MONTANA HISTORICAL SOCIETY, PAC2005-22AI P65G

gift. Their pleas explained that their library's situation in a small space far from the city center rendered it deficient. Funding from Carnegie would provide "a great good . . . in this remote place." James Bertram, Carnegie's secretary, finally replied favorably on January 19, 1905, offering $10,000 if the city agreed to the usual resolution for support and a suitable site. Throughout Lewistown, the long-awaited announcement "was the cause of much rejoicing."

In addition to the perfunctory language required by the gift, the Lewistown City Council issued an additional resolution on July 7, 1905, thanking Carnegie for his generosity, which would "be the means of affording the citizens of Lewistown many valuable privileges of a literary and educational nature and the Council particularly on behalf of the children and youth of this city, assures Mr. Carnegie that this gift will be used as to derive therefrom the greatest possible good for its beneficiaries."

By that time librarian Mary Sloan had resigned, and the library moved again, this time to the city hall. Sloan's replacement, Mrs. Albert Pfaus, accommodated patrons three afternoons per week while the city officials moved ahead with securing the lots and an architect. They accepted wealthy businessman T. C. Power's offer of lots two blocks from the commercial corridor at Fourth and Washington Streets, but then decided the lots were too remote and too expensive. In July, with the building site still up in the air, the *Argus* editors warned that Carnegie's offer might be in jeopardy and to "not let the opportunity to secure a splendid library building pass us by simply because we were unable to secure a site." Less than two weeks later, the editors rejoiced that their appeal "was not in vain. It only needed a little rustling. . . . A deed and abstract to two lots on upper Main Street having been procured and turned over to Mr. F. E. Smith, chairman of

▲ Details like the four-pointed carved stone capitals (left) and terra-cotta laurel swags (right) on the front of the library created a beautiful entrance but resulted in cost overruns. Though their original contract was for $10,000, the Tubb Brothers' final cost was $14,000.

the library board, . . . there should be but little delay before active work on the building is commenced."

In September 1905, local contractors, the Tubb Brothers, offered the sole bid to design and construct the building on the lots at the corner of Main Street and Seventh Avenue, across from the county courthouse. The Tubbs laid the cornerstone on October 31, 1905, and employed Croatian master stonemasons. Their cut sandstone and terra-cotta Neoclassical Revival design evolved through the building process to include many details and "extras." They completed the handcrafted edifice in August 1906 at a cost overrun of $4,000, but Jeff Tubb took the loss, saying, "I built that building according to what I thought was best and I will not accept one cent more than the contract price."

Perched on the hill overlooking the city from the west end of town, the one-story building on a daylight basement faced Main Street and was modest only in size—fifty feet across by twenty-four feet deep, with a semicircular extension on the rear (south) elevation. Exquisitely constructed, the library displayed uncoursed,

rough-cut sandstone, a hipped roof supported by carved brackets, and applied terra-cotta laurel swags. Oak doors led into a shallow vestibule that opened onto a central patron service area with reading rooms to either side. Stacks set in a fan pattern filled the rear extension. Below, the basement level provided clubrooms.

For lack of furnishings, the lovely building awaited use until February 1907, when librarian Archie Farnum began service to the city. Unfortunately, as had happened in Great Falls, the cost of furnishing, heating, and lighting exceeded the budget. The library closed in February 1908, and Farnum resigned. At the end of the year, Mrs. Pfaus accepted the appointment as full-time librarian and restored service. When she resigned in 1913, the city hired Mrs. Wait for a short tenure, then Clara Mondon Main took charge.

A former teacher and trained librarian, Main soon cataloged the collection and improved access for patrons. Over the next three years, both the number of volumes and library patronage increased. The building became overcrowded, and the need for a separate children's space became clear. After World War I, the city addressed the

▲ The builder's intricate craftsmanship is still evident inside today, where the swag laurels from the entry reappear in carved window trim. Ornate carved oak pillars mark the central foyer, flanked by two symmetrical reading rooms.

problem in part by converting the basement rooms for the "little folks." Despite the financial and space issues, Main insisted on expanding services and advocated to extend the library's reach by establishing a county library system. She was tirelessly active in serving patrons and provided leadership within the Montana Library Association as well. She retired in 1941, after nearly three decades of hard work.

Several librarians served as director during the tumultuous years following Main's retirement. In 1950, the board elevated Elizabeth Pittman to the position, a graduate of the University of Denver Library School. Pittman's long administration marked an important milestone: a much-needed expansion, made possible by a substantial bequest from Dena Busch. Dedicated on May 15, 1960, architect Chandler Cohagen's design added twenty-one hundred square feet at the basement level. Distinctly modern, the Busch Memorial Addition featured banks of aluminum-frame windows and an accessible entrance from Seventh Avenue.

As the building expanded, cries for countywide service did as well. Neither Pittman, who retired in 1969, nor her successor, Norma Kay Isern, were able to convince the county commissioners to commit to the idea. The issue came to a head amid funding crises during the late 1970s, and the county acquiesced in 1979. In 1990, the library underwent another extensive expansion and renovation that added forty-two hundred square feet to the first floor. The majority of library functions were consolidated into the daylight basement. With a design that strove to retain as much historic integrity as possible, the massive addition left the upper exterior relatively untouched, though

▲ In 1990, a substantial addition increased the Lewistown Carnegie library's footprint at street level. The modern addition offered 4,200 square feet of space and left the library's original main level intact. The addition's terraced roof now serves as an outdoor plaza.

it did encompass nearly all the lots' green space, and the addition's roof became the library plaza. Upstairs the reading rooms and circulation area were turned into dedicated meeting and museum spaces, with many of the original finishes revealed and restored.

This melding of new and old at the Lewistown Public Library is an excellent metaphor for the services the remarkable staff provide and the collections they protect. At the forefront of digitization projects, in recent years they have taken the lead in collecting and preserving manuscripts, photos, and memories from central Montana.

2122 — Carnegie Library — Glasgow, Mont.

GLASGOW

THE VAST GRASSLANDS ALONG THE MISSOURI, Poplar, and Milk River valleys in northeastern Montana are the homeland of the Blackfeet, Great Sioux, and Assiniboine Nations. By the late 1800s, however, the US government had forced most tribal members to live on reservations that represented a mere fraction of their traditional territory. The federal government reduced reservation lands across Montana Territory's northern tier in 1887 and 1888, largely to make way for the St. Paul, Minneapolis, and Manitoba Railway. After construction began from Minot, North Dakota, in 1887, railroad president James Hill observed Siding 45—the forty-fifth railroad siding west of Minot—and chose to locate a division point there. Named after the Scottish city of Glasgow, the community mushroomed over the next several years and in 1893 became the county seat of newly formed Valley County. It was incorporated in 1903, and

the population doubled from 500 to 1,158 in the first decade of the twentieth century, motivating residents to establish civic institutions and services.

Hoping to offer a place where the many single young men of the community could spend quality time, a handful of Glasgow residents formed the Glasgow Public Library and Reading Room Association in 1904. For two years, the association membership and private donations paid for rented space in a commercial building downtown and for librarian Elizabeth Wafford's salary. The library collections and use increased substantially, and the town residents voted to support the library via a tax levy in 1906. The first's year's levy reaped more than $600 in revenue. Pleased but still concerned about the library's future, association members sought to "clinch the safety of the library by establishing it so firmly that it would be out of the question to propose any measure for the repeal of any

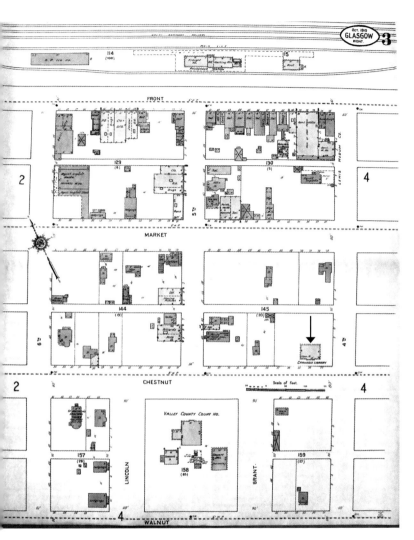

To be eligible for a Carnegie library gift, a community had to prove that it had secured a suitable site for the building. In Glasgow, the city purchased a site in the heart of the town at the corner of Chestnut and 4th, half a block over from the Valley County Courthouse. IMAGE COURTESY OF THE MONTANA HISTORICAL SOCIETY LIBRARY, GLASGOW SANBORN MAP, SHEET 3, 1910.

ordinance now standing." The association officers wrote to Andrew Carnegie on March 4, 1907, making clear their view that a Carnegie library gift would all but guarantee the library's future.

James Bertram, Carnegie's secretary, responded favorably, offering $7,500 for the Glasgow library. In exchange for the gift, Carnegie required that the city provide a suitable building site and allocate at least $750 annually—Carnegie's standard 10 percent of the gift amount—for library operations. The Glasgow Town Council resolved to do so on May 15, 1907, and two months later purchased four lots on the corner of Chestnut and Fourth Street South. Situated across from the new county courthouse, the library would be a few blocks from the commercial district.

The city council then called for architectural design bids and in October 1907 selected Chicago architect George W. Ashby's design. Vice president of the Radford Architectural Company, Ashby specialized in popular catalogs of standardized building plans. He offered Glasgow plans for a one-story brick-and-stone building on a raised basement, "with oak finish, oak and maple floors, gas and electric fixtures, mosaic work and nickel plumbing." The design was refined through the winter months and was executed by local contractor Dan McKay in the spring and summer of 1908. Montana's first Carnegie library to fully embrace the Carnegie Classic architectural ideal, the formal but restrained Neoclassical Revival edifice boasted a pedimented central entry flanked by wide pilasters, which also appeared at the corners and between the window openings on the side and rear elevations. A polished sandstone cornice highlighted the deep eaves of the building's hipped roof, and a rough-cut stone belt course functioned as the water table. Two sets of large

CARNEGIE PUBLIC LIBRARY.

▲ Completed in 1909 for $7,500, the Glasgow Carnegie library featured large, symmetrical windows on either side of a wide entry. Chicago architect George Ashby created pilasters, rather than columns, to highlight the simple entry. IMAGE COURTESY OF THE MONTANA HISTORICAL SOCIETY, PAC 2005-22AIP74D

▲ Before the construction of the Fort Peck Dam, Glasgow experienced several floods, as shown here (library pictured at far right) in June 1923. Though the library's basement level was vulnerable, the raised main floor generally remained well above the water line. IMAGE COURTESY OF THE MONTANA HISTORICAL SOCIETY, PAC 2013-50 1554

▲ A rare interior view of the Glasgow Carnegie library's Western Memorial Room, complete with a fireplace and furnishings by the influential western furniture designer Thomas C. Molesworth, ca. 1950. IMAGE COURTESY MONTANA HISTORICAL SOCIETY PAC 2002-3 BI

fundraisers hosted by staff and supporters. By 1918, Glasgow claimed nearly four thousand residents, and librarian Frances MacDonald welcomed nearly a quarter of that population into the library each month. Under the direction of librarian Sophia Bowling, appointed in 1920, the library flourished, serving approximately two thousand patrons each month through the subsequent decades. Despite statewide drought and economic uncertainty, library services rarely faltered through the 1920s and 1930s.

Bowling served in the Glasgow Public Library until she retired in 1945 at the age of eighty-eight. That year marked a significant transition for the library, not only because of Bowling's departure but also because its mission expanded to include countywide services. Led by the newly hired librarian, Georgia Dignan, the collections and patronage continued to grow. Serving not only the entirety of Valley County, the library staff also often attended to the needs of other northeastern Montana counties. As the responsibilities and collections grew, the original Carnegie library building proved insufficient. By the early 1960s, library staff and local citizens began clamoring for an updated facility and additional space.

The early 1960s was a heady time in Glasgow. Expansion of the nearby Glasgow Air Force Base resulted in an influx of residents and stimulated the local economy. Glasgow's modernist architectural landscape, including the county

windows appeared across each elevation, while pairs of smaller windows lit the basement area. The interior featured a central "librarian's station" with a "reading and writing room" to each side. The basement contained the standard meeting room and children's reading room.

The library opened with great fanfare in July 1909. The collection and patrons increased steadily over the next several years. In the early 1910s, ongoing library improvement projects included repairs, redecoration, and sidewalks, paid for by a two mill library levy and

▲ For many communities, having a Carnegie public library was a point of pride, as shown by this ca. 1920 postcard. Sadly, the Glasgow library was demolished in 1965. IMAGE COURTESY OF THE MONTANA HISTORICAL SOCIETY, PAC 2005-22AI P74D

courthouse and the Glasgow City-County Library, reflects this prosperity. Valley County and Glasgow city officials agreed to move forward with new library building plans in 1965. The Montana State Library promised matching money, supplied by Library Services and Construction Act funds, to build the proposed $88,000 facility. The city demolished the Glasgow Carnegie library in September 1965, constructing a much larger and decidedly modern building in its place. Whereas the historic library perched in the center of four landscaped lots, the New Formalist-style building designed by local architect G. E. Kjelstrup

filled the south half of the parcel, with a large parking lot to the rear. Though less graceful and inviting than the original Carnegie library, the new building did provide better access—not only to people who had difficulty managing stairs but also for the large trucks used in the five-county bookmobile program. It was dedicated on May 29, 1966.

The Glasgow City-County Library became the hub of information services when it was chosen as the headquarters for the Golden Plains Library Federation in Montana in 1973. Today, the Glasgow City-County Library continues its original mission of serving northeastern Montana.

BIG TIMBER

W HEN BIG TIMBER WAS INCORPORATED IN 1902, THE early townsfolk's politics tended toward the progressive. Local women's groups and other civic-minded organizations wanted to cure social ills and pledged to pursue "the advancement, betterment and general welfare of our town." The city council soon voted in favor of several municipal improvements for "a bigger, better and more beautiful Big Timber," to "keep pace with other progressive cities in the state." Among these was a public library.

W. S. Eastman, a representative from the H. Parmelee Library Company, a subscription library service based in Iowa, convinced many Big Timber residents to purchase a library membership for $5 and pay an additional $1 each year to use a collection of 1,000 books supplied and regularly rotated by the company. The "branch library" opened in February 1901 and operated from J. Cameron's store in town.

But rather than depend on the out-of-state service over the long term, locals decided to initiate plans for Big Timber's own public library. In 1904, the local Congregational church offered space for the venture, including reading rooms. Materials could be checked out by persons who paid $1 for a library card. Established by the city in 1905, the Big Timber Library Association joined forces with the Big Timber Women's Club's Library Auxiliary committee to fundraise for the library's permanent home, but it took six years before the town was ready to make a request to Andrew Carnegie. During most of that time, the Knights of Pythias Hall housed the library, and Elizabeth "Bessie" H. Moore served as librarian and library association secretary, while J. A. Lowry served as president.

Meanwhile, the Women's Club's Library Auxiliary continued to fundraise and had enough money to purchase

Completed in 1914 at a cost of $7,500, the Big Timber Carnegie Public Library features a red brick main floor and a daylight basement clad with local river rock. IMAGE COURTESY MONTANA HISTORICAL SOCIETY, PAC 2013-50 BI B9965

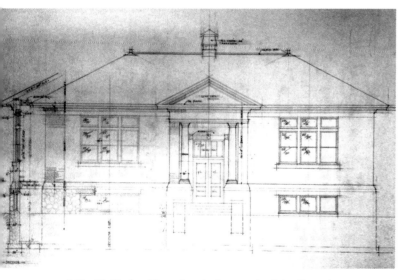

The Big Timber Library is a classic example of the Carnegie Corporation's "Floor Plan A" and was designed by the Link and Haire architectural firm. IMAGE COURTESY OF MONTANA STATE UNIVERSITY ARCHIVES COLLECTION 1103, DRAWING SET 013.

lots for a library in the autumn of 1909. On March 26, 1911, Lowry wrote to Carnegie, "The people of Big Timber and surrounding country are quite enthusiastic for a building, and trust that you can see your way clear to aid us in erecting a building that will be an honor to the town and those who aided in building it."

Carnegie's secretary, James Bertram, wrote to Lowry in May 1911, offering a $7,500 bequest for a library building, with the familiar conditions that the town establish a levy for building maintenance and secure a suitable building lot. Just a month later, the town enacted Ordinance 89 to establish and maintain a free public library. Lowry wrote again requesting sample plans for a $7,500 library, and Bertram responded with information to "give you a general idea of what the arrangement should be." But the good progress soon hit a snag, as the townspeople and various committees could not agree on the most suitable lot. Correspondence between Lowry and Bertram during spring 1912 revealed both men's frustration. Lowry explained in September 1912: "I presume you think it strange that I am doing so much writing with seemingly no advancement toward a library building. But the fact of the matter is this—the writer together with several others thot [sic] that we had a very desirable location . . . but others thot [sic] differently. . . . It took us all this time in securing the new location."

When Lowry wrote again in February 1913, he noted a corner lot had been purchased, and Bertram sent plans for a $7,500 library recently constructed in Colfax, Iowa. Five months later, Lowry finally submitted plans for the library building at Big Timber. Charles Haire, who designed Carnegie libraries for Dillon, Great Falls, Bozeman, and Miles City, partnered with John Gustave Link in 1906, and together they designed many significant buildings

▲ Link and Haire offered a simple but elegant design for Big Timber featuring a pedimented entry with Doric columns beneath boxed and dentiled eaves.

▲ A portrait of Andrew Carnegie offers silent approval to the newly expanded and remodeled circulation area of the Carnegie Public Library in Big Timber.

across the state. As Bertram had suggested, their drawings for the Big Timber library resembled the restrained Neoclassical Revival design of the Colfax, Iowa, Carnegie library, and its floor plan closely matched Bertram's suggested "Plan A" as published in the Carnegie Corporation of New York's "Notes on the Erection of Library Bildings" [*sic*]. Bertram approved the plans in August, and by early fall Lowry was ready to move forward with construction.

Local contractors Gagnon and Company won the $7,500 construction bid. By January 20, 1914, they had completed the shell of the library building, but the interior remained unfinished, and costs exceeded the allowable $7,500. Even though the Big Timber Women's Club agreed to fund the basement finishes, Lowry was forced to ask Bertram for an additional $1,000 "for the heating of the building." Bertram declined. Lowry and his colleagues

▲ Generous collections and reading spaces flooded with natural light remain integral features of the Big Timber Carnegie Public Library today.

eventually found alternative funding and installed a boiler to heat the library.

The new Big Timber Carnegie Public Library, "a handsome, stone and brick structure," finally opened in March 1914. Librarian Lena Clark reported statistics regularly, and patronage and collections expanded. Library users were welcome to check out books Tuesday, Thursday, and Saturday afternoons, but on Sundays, only the reading rooms were accessible. Mindful of Bertram's penchant for library grantees following the rules, Lowry continued to send him updates for another two years to be sure that the board membership and use of the building was in keeping with the Carnegie library guidelines.

In 1922 the Big Timber Library Board adopted a constitution and bylaws. At the same time, they developed policies governing the operation of the library. Six years later, the Sweetgrass County Commission approved an annual contribution to support the library's operation. Over the next several decades, the library continued to serve the city and surrounding communities with its collections and programming. Throughout the twentieth century,

the Big Timber Women's Club remained integral to the operation and use of the library: the members met in the basement room, sponsored lectures and fundraisers, promoted Library Week events, and conducted a children's reading hour. Reflecting on the library's 1966 annual report, the *Big Timber Pioneer* concluded that, "in spite of television, radio, and stereo, some folks still read." That year, the library held 12,700 volumes, and the following year it expanded its service area when it became the city-county library.

Edna Goosey began her tenure as head librarian during the early 1970s, and "one of her greatest joys [was] watching students develop and maintain an interest in the printed word." She noted the need for additional space, particularly for students, and promoted the idea of moving some of the collections into the meeting room. Her initiative culminated in a $5,000 basement renovation, completed in 1975 that provided new shelving, fresh paint, and the installation of a drop ceiling and carpeting. In 2001, the library planning committee and library director Lauren McMullen began to investigate options for expansion. Thanks to generous donations, in 2007 the library gained an addition and addressed long-needed improvements, such as new technology, additional space, and upgraded accessibility.

Since 1914, the Big Timber Carnegie Public Library has functioned as an information center and meeting place. A testament to the progressive-minded leaders of the community, the library and its staff continue to offer the city and county outreach programs, community events, and access to technology, as well as providing reading and research materials. The building—both the original structure and its mirror-image addition—is an architectural and cultural anchor in Big Timber, representative of the understated yet enduring community it serves.

▲ Completed in 2007, the Big Timber Carnegie Public Library's addition doubled the library's space. The new building closely resembled the original in style and form as seen by the original entrance (top) and the new accessible entrance of the addition (bottom).

HAVRE

In 1879, the United States Army established Fort Assinniboine just south of the Milk River. Over the next decade, traders at the fort founded businesses six miles northeast, at Bullhook Bottoms. The Great Northern Railway carved its way across Montana during the late 1880s, and by 1890 the company had invested in the town as a division point. Renamed Havre, the town began to flourish through the 1890s. With infrastructure came families, and by 1900, nearly three thousand people called Havre home.

While the fort maintained a thousand-volume library, the city lacked a publicly accessible institution. In 1901, Havre's populace began to advocate for a city library and reading room, not only for access to information but also to show "the outside world that the mayor and aldermen plan better things for Havre and do not dream them all day long." As in other communities, the local women's club took up the mantle, creating a public library by encouraging its fifty members to donate twenty-five cents a month to the cause.

In 1904, the city established a library board, and the Havre Women's Club, led by Harriet Bossuot, Mrs. J. C. Pancoast, Margaret Clack, and Sadie Broadwater, organized the official Havre Public Library, opening it on January 1, 1905. They operated it each afternoon and evening from the Security Bank's basement room. By 1907, the holdings consisted of more than fifteen hundred items, and the library moved to larger accommodations in the city hall. The Havre City Council approved ongoing funding in 1911 and hired Lillian Hammond as the city's first paid librarian. At the same time, the Havre Women's Club began in earnest to try to secure a Carnegie library building for the community. The club donated $600 toward the city's December 1912 purchase of corner lots designated for a library at Fourth Avenue and Fifth Street.

▲ Architect Marion Riffo created a Neoclassical Revival design for the Havre Carnegie library in 1913. Tall pairs of windows provided ample natural light to the main floor and daylight basement.

▲ Riffo's castellated roof line made of Hebron brick and cast concrete coping remains a distinctive feature of the building today.

As chair of the Havre Women's Club library committee, Harriet Bossuot initiated the application process with the Carnegie Corporation of New York in January 1913. Secretary James Bertram offered Havre a grant of $12,000 on March 14, with the standard stipulation that the city pass a resolution establishing a local tax to generate at least 10 percent of the donated amount annually. The city quickly complied, forwarding news of a resolution to Bertram the following month and putting out a call for plans and bids. Dissatisfied with the architects' drawings submitted through the summer of 1913, Havre's city officials continued their search until the end of the year.

Havre ultimately chose Kalispell architect Marion Riffo's design. In July 1914, Bertram approved the now-familiar rectangular one-story and daylight basement building in the Neoclassical Revival style. Constructed of blond Hebron brick and highlighted with terra-cotta detailing, a castellated parapet, a thick stepped cornice, and a pedimented entry, the forty-by-sixty-foot building offered a sophisticated presence. A pair of oak one-light doors provided entry, and the multi-light glass-block transom above filtered sunshine into the vestibule. Large pairs of windows topped with transoms dominated the library's west façade and provided ample natural light to the main floor. A pair of reading rooms flanked a central circulation desk and reference area. The finished basement held meeting rooms, where the women's club met regularly.

Head librarian Mary Homan, together with assistant librarian and women's club member Emlyn Benson and volunteers, directed the move of the library's 18,000 books and 410 records into the new space, and the library opened in November 1914. Homan guided the library's growth over the next eight years, and Benson took the helm in 1922. Benson, who trained at the University of

▲ The large windows of Marion Riffo's original design flooded the interior with light, creating an ideal space for a modern-day art gallery.

Wisconsin and was an active member of the Montana Library Association, believed that libraries were not luxuries, but necessities: "Libraries are not supposed to be merely buildings with collections of dead and dusty books, but living agents for service."

Benson's tenure as head librarian lasted more than two decades, and she was responsible for an expansion of library holdings and services through years plagued by economic depression. Her special interest in encouraging young readers led her to team up with the Havre Women's Club and the Havre Parent-Teacher Association to open a designated children's room in the library's lower level in 1936. When she retired in 1944, the *Havre Daily News* observed: "Her record is outstanding and the entire community has benefitted from her unceasing efforts that have made the Havre Library one of the best in the state. She has spared neither time nor energy in rendering a great service."

Several people served as head librarian after Benson's retirement, until the library board appointed Mary Antunes, a Havre native and experienced librarian, to the position in 1953. Under her tenure, through the 1950s and '60s, the Havre Public Library expanded its collections, participated in the Montana State Library's cooperative services, provided children's programming, scheduled clubs and programs in the public meeting rooms, and hosted art exhibits and fundraisers. In the early 1970s, however, amid strained city and county budgets, Antunes began to call for a consolidation of the city and county libraries. She and county librarian Dorothy Armstrong agreed that combining the two libraries' resources would allow for expanded hours, collections, and services. They also emphasized the need for a larger, more easily accessible library building. Indeed, as the city and county pursued consolidation over the next decade, the problem of acquiring and paying for a space

 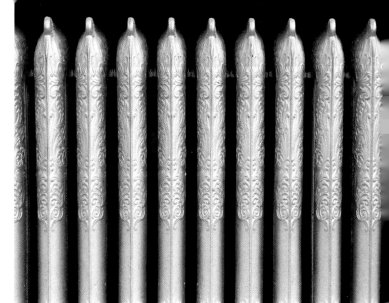

▲ Riffo's design for the Havre library offered additional ornamentation inside, including pressed-tin ceilings, crown moldings, and ornate radiators.

large enough to accommodate a city-county public library proved formidable.

Antunes retired in 1980, after twenty-seven years of service and before her vision of a combined city-county library was realized. Over the next five years, city librarian Bill Lisenby "laid the foundation for an integrated, harmonious library organization to serve all area patrons." In 1983, administration for the city and county libraries was consolidated, and fundraising began for a new building. Two years later, the owners of the former Havre Clinic building donated it for the library. Librarian Bonnie Williamson directed renovations of the large and accessible building, and the new consolidated library held its grand opening in June 1986. The 1914 Carnegie library building was left vacant.

Though the city chose to sell the original Carnegie property, it recognized the building's historic significance and encouraged prospective buyers to maintain its archi-

tectural integrity. Havre resident Kathy Shirilla purchased the Carnegie library building in April 1986, the sole bidder at the city's auction. Careful to keep the library's original design intact, including the original finishes and many of the bookshelves, Shirilla restored and repurposed the library into the Old Library Gallery. As agent to beloved Havre artist Don Greytak, Shirilla has featured his work in the gallery from the start, as well as providing display and retail space to other artists from around the region.

The Havre-Hill County Library continues to thrive as well, offering a large collection of books, manuscripts, and archival material, digitized collections, community meeting space, classroom and presentation space, and a music room in its new home on Third Street. In addition to presiding over the formation of the consolidated library, librarian Bonnie Williamson also expanded programs, technology, and public outreach, earning her the Librarian of the Year Award in 1994.

▲ Today Havre's Old Library Gallery preserves the look and feel of the library by retaining the central library desk and original windows. Pictured behind the desk are gallery owner Kathy Shirilla and local artist Don Greytak.

HAMILTON

The River of the Red Willows—as the original indigenous inhabitants called what is now known as the Bitterroot River—carves its way through a verdant valley between the Bitterroot Range's ragged peaks to the west and the Sapphire Range's gentler slopes to the east. Here, innumerable generations of Salish lived: hunting, fishing, collecting plants for medicine and food, and participating in extensive trade networks in the region. Non-Indian explorers and trappers filtered through the valley in the first half of the nineteenth century, and Jesuit missionaries, led by Father Pierre-Jean De Smet, established St. Mary's Mission in 1841. The 1855 Hellgate Treaty at Council Grove marked the beginning of the Salish bands' forced migration north to the Flathead Indian Reservation. As the nineteenth century progressed, more whites settled permanently in the valley.

Undoubtedly, many of those new arrivals brought private book collections with them. In 1861, Montana Anglo pioneers Granville and James Stuart traveled to the valley from their home in Deer Lodge—150 miles away—solely to purchase books left behind by a trader. Father Anthony Ravalli maintained a small private library in his quarters at St. Mary's Mission, and John Owen had an excellent collection at his fort and trading post near Stevensville. Copper magnate Marcus Daly and his wife, Margaret, maintained a large private library at their sprawling estate, Riverside. But the city of Hamilton, which Daly established in 1890, lacked a publicly accessible library through its first decade, despite exponential growth. By 1901 residents, including the *Western News* editor, were calling for reading rooms and book circulation, for the "educational advancement of the community." Hamiltonian P. D. Schipperus expanded on that lofty sentiment, declaring libraries to be essential for "mental

▲ Erick Trosdahl's design allowed for three evenly spaced windows on each side of the front door. As with the design for many Carnegie libraries, the smaller side windows are set high to allow room for bookcases.
IMAGE COURTESY OF MONTANA HISTORICAL SOCIETY, PAC 2013-50 HAMI BLDGS 26

and moral judgement . . . good citizenship [and to] kill the hissing snakes of anarchy." While the clamor for a library continued, progress stalled until January 1903, when the Hamilton Ministerial Association proposed a one-mill city tax levy for library purposes. The money, when combined with donations, would form "the nucleus of a library" and put the municipality in good stead to approach Andrew Carnegie for a gift. While the city contemplated the levy, the association set up a small library of donated books in the Ravalli County Bank and offered access through subscription. In August, after a successful public vote, the city appointed a library committee in anticipation of the first tax money becoming available in December 1903. By February 1904, the library was "flourishing," boasting more than one thousand books ready for circulation. The

collection moved to a room within the newly constructed city hall in 1907 and was made available to the public.

Carrie Pond, who was recently widowed, began her career as Hamilton city librarian in November 1910, working from the 740-square-foot library room in the city hall. The same month, the city's chamber of commerce wrote to Carnegie's secretary, James Bertram, to request funds for a library building, but the lack of a building site caused the process to stall. The idea to apply for a Carnegie grant surfaced again three years later, and this time, the Hamilton Women's Club was determined not to let the opportunity pass. Noting the quality of the local population and the poor library accommodations—a room adjacent to the horse stalls—Mrs. J. F. Sullivan, chair of the club's library committee, wrote to Bertram in March 1914. The city library board, in partnership with the women's club, then submitted an application that met with quick approval and $9,000 from Bertram. Margaret Daly, the widow of "Copper King" Marcus Daly and owner of the Valley Mercantile Company, donated lots west of the city hall for the library site.

The city chose library plans submitted by local contractor Erick Trosdahl, a "thoroughly conscientious, honest Swede [he was actually Norwegian] . . . having either contracted or superintended the construction of most of the best buildings in the city." Bertram called for changes, particularly the location of the basement stairwell, the lower-level ceiling height, and the "large entrance feature"; he approved a revised version in March 1915. In late July, Trosdahl won the construction bid as well. His crew excavated and set the foundation in September and began laying the brickwork in October. By December, the reserved rectangular building with Neoclassical Revival style detailing was nearly ready for occupancy.

▲ The Hamilton Carnegie library was designed and constructed in the Neoclassical Revival style by local builder Erick Trosdahl.

▲ Now protected by a gabled overhang, the Hamilton library's original entry included a stepped brickwork pediment.

Trosdahl's design, left less ornate by Bertram's refusal of an extended entry, called for dark red pressed brick, a hipped roof covered in slate, bracketed boxed eaves, and a raised concrete basement clad in stucco. A short staircase led to the façade's center entry, which was highlighted by narrow pilasters and a stepped brickwork pediment set below the eaves. The interior followed the Carnegie Corporation's recommendations for a central circulation area flanked by stacks and reading rooms, with a meeting room in the basement.

By the following April, the proper furniture had not arrived, and sidewalk construction was still underway. In June, faults in the sidewalk delayed the opening another month. The library finally opened in July 1916, and Carrie Pond settled in to serve the community: "As city librarian Mrs. Pond was one of Hamilton's most notable citizens.

▲ Completed in 1916, the Hamilton Carnegie library features bracketed eaves.

Her guidance in reading had been given to three generations. She saw the library progress from a corner in city hall to the modern Carnegie establishment which was her pride. . . . Mrs. Pond had perhaps helped more young people to the ideals of life than any other resident during her more than half a century here."

Under Pond, the library's circulation remained steady, averaging about two thousand books checked out each month, and patrons included not only city residents but also outlying community members willing to pay a fee. The Hamilton Women's Club met there monthly and supported the library through fundraisers and events, including rallying for a children's library and book purchases. The club's garden committee also helped with the library's

grounds, which expanded to include the block's entire southwest corner by the early 1930s.

Pond died in November 1944, and Mrs. Floy Fitzgerald, "one of Hamilton's best-known women," took her place in December. Over her fifteen-year tenure, the library hours expanded, and the city increased its library levy to two mills. The Five Valleys Federation of Libraries, created in the mid-1950s, offered bookmobile services, shared collections between libraries, and gave financial assistance to improve collections and the appearance of buildings. The Hamilton Public Library benefitted from a renovation in 1960, and services and collections increased over the next two decades under the direction of librarians Ruth Flightner and Lucille Gordon.

In the early 1980s, discussions began between the city and county to officially expand the library's mission to include the Hamilton, Corvallis, and Victor School Districts. These discussions coincided with a major capital campaign to build a large library addition. The library, renamed the Bitterroot Pubic Library in 1987, reached its $307,500 goal with city, county, state, and federal money, together with private donations, and opened the enlarged library in February 1988. Attached to the rear of the original Carnegie building and compatible in design, the addition nearly tripled the usable square footage.

Since then, the Bitterroot Public Library has continued to increase its technological capabilities, provide literacy services and children's programming, and participate in statewide and regional cooperative curricula. Though some changes have occurred inside and out, the Carnegie library building in Hamilton has provided space for reading, learning, and community events for over a century and promises to do so well into the future.

▲ The Hamilton Carnegie library's basement entrance required visitors to descend stairs for access. The 1987–88 remodel added an alternate doorway, reached via ramp, and an elevator between floors inside.

▲ Though fully modernized today, the original Carnegie floor plan remains intact, its windows offering ample light above collections space.

▲ Originally designed for community meetings, the library basement now offers staff plenty of work and storage space.

MALTA

THE STORY GOES THAT MALTA, MONTANA, GOT ITS name when a railroad official spun a globe of the world and his finger landed on the island of Malta in the Mediterranean Sea. But before it was Malta, the location was Siding 54 on the St. Paul, Minneapolis, and Manitoba Railway. There, Canadian-born Robert Trafton took up land and set up a mercantile business after following the railroad's construction crews across Montana's Hi-Line in 1887. In 1890, Trafton became the location's first postmaster. The city incorporated in 1909, the year of the Enlarged Homestead Act. As more families arrived, they established social and civic clubs, and in 1910 "public-minded citizens," including members of the Malta Women's Club, started a library. Mabel Peck served as volunteer librarian and circulated donated books and magazines from the office of the local newspaper, the *Enterprise*. Three years later, the women's club assumed control, and moved the operation to Murray's Drug Store, where Ethel Murray acted as librarian.

Malta was named the county seat when Phillips County was established in 1915, an event that coincided with a national and statewide movement to create county libraries. A proponent of Montana's proposed County Library Law, Montana State University (now the University of Montana in Missoula) librarian Gertrude Buckhous used the strong voice of the state's women's clubs to rally support, leading to the law's quick and successful implementation. Phillips County was one of the first to embrace it, together with Chouteau and Blaine Counties. Over the winter and spring of 1916, Catherine Kilduff and many other area club members crossed the countryside collecting the requisite 20 percent of county taxpayers' signatures on a petition to create the county library. The petition carried, and the county appointed Kilduff to the first library board in November. That year she also actively pursued a Carnegie gift for a library building. Carnegie Corporation Secretary James Bertram offered the county $15,000 in December 1916.

▲ Havre-based architect Frank Bossuot designed a Neoclassical Revival style Carnegie library for Malta. Note the hinged fanlight transoms, allowing for ventilation during the hot prairie summers.
IMAGE COURTESY MONTANA HISTORICAL SOCIETY, PAC 2005-22 AIP3

▲ The fanlight and pediment above the front door of the Phillips County Carnegie library were the most ornate features of the new building. Pressed-metal details conveyed classical inspiration.

Robert Tratton, the early postmaster, offered the site of his initial residence in the area for the library, four lots at the west end of Front Street. The county engaged Havre architect Frank Bossuot to design the building. Not only did Bossuot bring his experience in civic architecture—including the Hill County Courthouse and the Phillips County Jail—but he also could tap into the advice of his wife, Harriet, who had worked to make the Havre Carnegie library a reality. Bossuot's vision, within Bertram's demanding standards, translated into a restrained Neoclassical Revival building of tan brick.

Like Montana's other Carnegie libraries, Phillips County's building would be one story on a raised basement. The balanced façade featured a pedimented and pilastered entry flush with the elevation, with a fanlight above paired oak doors. Fanlight transoms, hinged so they could be opened for circulation during the hot summers, topped each of the four pairs of large windows set across the front's main level as well as the recessed brick panels, meant to hint at openings, across the side and rear walls. Pressed-metal details—including the pediment, belt courses, and medallions—conveyed classical inspiration. In the interior, the main story's open plan accommodated a central circulation desk with reading rooms and open stacks to either side. The basement level below included a lecture room, offices, and bathroom facilities.

In November 1917, less than a year after Carnegie's offer of support, the Malta Women's Club transferred its eight-hundred-book collection in the drugstore to the county, under the care of librarian Mildred Scott. Trained by Buckhous, and an assistant at the Chouteau County Library, Scott had the expertise to implement the new county library model in Malta. On January 9, 1918, the state's first purpose-built county library building opened as the Phillips County Library. The following year, Scott reported that her efforts had proved highly successful; both in town and across the county, "interest and enthusiasm [were] unanimous and very sincere." The collection and number of branch libraries steadily increased through Scott's tenure and continued to do so after Mary Fuller Homan took over the job in 1921.

Homan's efficiency and dedication to service transformed the Phillips County Library into a model institution. Though agriculture and the economy suffered greatly in the 1920s, on Homan's watch the number of branches and stations increased from nine in 1919 to eighty-eight in 1928. The county's collection grew to more than seven thousand volumes by the end of the 1920s, dispersed to the public from the Malta headquarters in person, through distribution centers, and via a book truck. Library enthusiast and county-area booster Mattie T. Cramer, a pioneer homesteader and newspaperwoman, gushed: "Progress made during the past decade places [the library] with the distinguished and spectacular, so great has been its achievements."

In 1933, the county's economic woes forced Homan to endure a 40 percent salary cut—from $100 to $60 per month—in order to keep the library operating. By 1936, the library's guiding forces, Homan and Catherine Kilduff, had passed away, and the library entered a new phase. With a "pleasant face and friendly personality," Eunice Ward began her twenty-year tenure in 1941. Despite a decrease in the number of branches and a fall in the county population, the library remained popular: it provided a respite from troubled times and a source of information about the latest agricultural techniques and news.

In the 1960s librarian Viola Bergen began the library's transition to cooperative regional service, and Evelyn

▲ A shallow parapet wall gave the Phillips County Carnegie library the appearance of additional height, while details such as dentils and small cast ornaments were in line with the Neoclassical Revival style.

▲ Today the Phillips County Carnegie library sits empty, and new owners hope to repurpose it as a community center.

▲ The Malta open floor plan featured a staircase with handcrafted wood railings leading to the basement level from near the circulation desk.

Brandt took charge in 1972. The next year the State Library Extension Commission formed the Golden Plains Library Federation. Funded first by a federal grant, Phillips was one of four counties that voted to support the network in 1973. Though funding for services continued to be a struggle, the county voters were convinced that the Carnegie library building no longer functioned appropriately, because of its lack of accessibility and outdated systems, and they supported a bond for a new library in 1977. The octagon-shaped building opened on May 8, 1978, and offered an open floor plan, accessible entrance, more square footage, and designated technology and children's areas. County offices also occupied part of the basement. Set on welcoming grassy lots at Fourth Street and Central Avenue, the library surged in popularity over the next four decades, as classes, technology, and children's programming expanded.

Meanwhile, the Phillips County Historical Society converted the Phillips County Carnegie library into a museum and succeeded in getting the building listed in the National Register of Historic Places in 1980. Unfortunately, the museum moved in 1996, leaving the building vacant and unmaintained until Mark and Tana Oyler purchased it at auction twelve years later. The Oylers stabilized the property but were unable to fully restore it. In 2016, Norris, Montana residents Kim Hudson and Rachel Liff were driving around Malta and discovered the beautiful building boarded up and falling into disrepair. Determined to save it, they purchased the building and now hope to revitalize it as a community center for meetings, events, and lodging. Their success would help preserve this remarkable and truly significant edifice, so it could continue to serve the area for many decades to come.

▲ The Carnegie library in Malta displayed elegant lighting fixtures and pressed-tin ceilings throughout the main floor.

FORT BENTON

Dorothy McLeish, together with several other prominent women in her community, founded the Fort Benton Study Club in October 1914. As its president, McLeish intended for Chouteau County to be the first in the state to take advantage of the newly passed Montana County Library Law. To this end, she wrote to the Carnegie Corporation's secretary, James Bertram, in July 1915. She explained that though the club had successfully petitioned the county for a half-mill library levy, "if we do not get a library building through philanthropy, we will ne're have one for a good many years." She also stated that her husband, A. E. McLeish, would donate two lots on which to build.

When the county commissioners followed up with Bertram in September 1915, they were confident that they would receive a promise relatively quickly, as the funding prerequisites of a levy and a lot were already in place. The commissioners completed Bertram's application as best they could, explaining that because of changes to the county boundaries, they could only estimate the county population and tax base. Over the course of the next six months, correspondence, reassurances, and explanations from university librarian Gertrude Buckhous sorted out the issue. Finally, Bertram promised to take the application forward.

The Carnegie Corporation of New York approved the application, and Bertram informed County Clerk Lester M. Bond on March 31, 1916, of their intention to provide $15,000 for a library building. His communications included the standard specific instructions as to how to proceed. In May, former resident Joseph Hirshberg offered two lots at Main and Baker Streets for a building site, a more prominent location than A. E. McLeish's promised lots enjoyed. The county called for architects to submit plans for the building, and the political wrangling began.

▲ Helena architect George Carsley offered a Prairie style vision for the Fort Benton library, featuring a full-height entry with divided sidelights and square transoms. In 1994 the county added a full-height extension to the front foyer, covering the original entry. IMAGE COURTESY MONTANA HISTORICAL SOCIETY PAC 2002-3.

Factions within the county supported more than one architectural firm: both Claude and Starck, who built many public libraries in their home state of Wisconsin and elsewhere, and George Carsley, who had designed prominent buildings in Helena, submitted plans. Additional local discord arose regarding library personnel, and professionally trained county librarian Zoe F. Meade resigned. Bertram tried to stay above the fray, concentrating on having the proper paper work filed and offering comments on the floor plans.

In hopes that different county commissioners might improve the situation, Buckhous requested that Bertram delay final approval until after the next election. Bertram agreed. The new county commissioners decided to begin the library design process over again and sent Bertram new plans drawn by Carsley in December 1916. Bertram again took Buckhous's advice and said he would approve the plans. First, however, Bertram reminded the county that the required paperwork remained outstanding. In the spring and summer of 1917, the commissioners tackled the paperwork and hired librarian Pauline Madden. As Zoe Meade had done before, Madden operated the

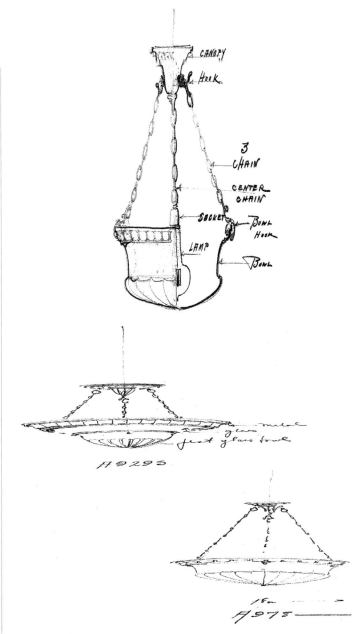

▲ Glass pendant lights with brass chains were specially designed for the reading rooms of the Carnegie Library in Fort Benton in 1918. IMAGE COURTESY CHOUTEAU COUNTY LIBRARY

▲ The original adult reading room is largely unchanged after a century of use, as seen here in 1918 and 2018. A brick fireplace and richly stained woodwork below large rectangular windows make an inviting area. The dropped ceiling (to accommodate modern heating, cooling, and electrical systems) and plastic pendant lights were added later. IMAGES COURTESY OF MONTANA HISTORICAL SOCIETY PAC 2002-3 BI AND TOM FERRIS.

library from rooms in the Masonic Hall, teaming with local individuals and women's club members to establish libraries countywide.

James Sherry, who built the Phillips County Carnegie library in Malta, won the construction bid in September. He was unable to proceed, however, because of the oncoming winter and the county commission's continued failure to find and complete the Carnegie paperwork. At long last, over the summer of 1918, Carsley's restrained, Prairie style-influenced design began to take shape. While adhering to the standard main-story and daylight basement layout, Carsley rejected the neoclassical details found on other Carnegie libraries across the state. Instead, he called for a low-slung hipped roof with deep, boxed eaves. The front elevation of the Hebron brick building featured tall windows beneath nearly square multi-light transoms. Unadorned shallow pilasters flanked the

full-height entry, and sidelights and transoms illuminated the unusually wide lobby. A reading room, complete with a brick fireplace, graced the southeast side, while stacks and a children's area filled the northwest. Richly stained bookcases lined the walls beneath the high windows. The basement contained a lecture room, a bathroom, storage space, and a packing area.

The Chouteau County Carnegie library finally opened on October 4, 1918, and the Fort Benton Women's Club, which had been integral to the library's founding and operation, held their inaugural season meeting in the new lecture room two days later. Just days after that, the Spanish flu arrived; the library was closed and opening celebrations delayed. Despite all of these troubles, county librarian Madden continued the work of creating a fully functioning library, reporting in August 1919 that the library had twenty-one branches and stations. When

▲ Carsley's classic layout for Fort Benton's library has survived numerous renovations, and still features a central entry flanked on either side by reading rooms.

▲ Today the children's area of the Chouteau County Library remains on the main floor in the original portion of the library, complete with the original bookcases below the high windows.

drought and economic depression plagued the state in the 1920s, that number decreased substantially. In 1931, Ellen Torgrimson was appointed county librarian and oversaw the six remaining branches.

Torgrimson remained county librarian for fifteen years and expanded the library's work countywide. She improved efficiency and outreach, kept abreast of national developments in library science, and served as president of the Montana Library Association. Together with Dorothy McLeish, she collaborated with the local women's club to continue to offer lectures and educational opportunities at the main branch at Fort Benton, other branches, and schools. Her retirement in 1945, as World War II was ending, was front-page news.

Torgrimson's departure coincided with postwar modernization and increased economic security. The library remained relevant, often contributing articles to local newspapers and hosting regular public events. In the 1980s, the issue of accessibility came to a head, and the

introduction of digital media further challenged the library. The county made the first major alterations to the library building in seventy years, adding an accessible entrance in 1988. In 1994, the county funded a major addition to the rear and a full-height extension across the façade. The addition blends with the original building, displaying a hipped roof, large sidelights and transoms, and matching Hebron brick. In addition to the extra space, the renovation provided the opportunity to install modern technology.

While some changes have occurred on the outside of the building, the Chouteau County Library remains largely unaltered inside. The original shelving and woodwork still grace the walls, patrons still read and gather around the fireplace, and the librarian still holds vigil at the central circulation desk. The Fort Benton Women's Club still holds its regular meetings in the downstairs lecture room—now named the McLeish Room—as it has for a hundred years. The modern yet familiar library undoubtedly will continue its unwavering service for decades to come.

▲ In 1988, the Chouteau County Library received a large rear addition, which included an accessible entrance.

HARDIN

THE CHICAGO, BURLINGTON, AND QUINCY RAILROAD (CB&Q) constructed its line through the Crow Indian Reservation in 1894, connecting its terminus at Sheridan, Wyoming, with the Northern Pacific line in Billings. Almost immediately, the railroad and eager settlers pressured the US government to make a deal with the Crow Nation to give up even more of its land. The Crow agreed to cede more than one million acres in exchange for payment, and an April 27, 1904 Act of Congress made it official. CB&Q's townsite firm, the Lincoln Land Company, quickly purchased the land that would become Hardin, platted its streets, and began to sell lots by May 1907. That summer, businesses and settlers began to build up the town. Within three years, Hardin boasted a population of 515, as well as numerous commercial enterprises. What it lacked, however, was an abundance of cultural and social amenities familiar to the new population.

Determined to remedy the situation, several women in town founded the Ladies Commercial Club in 1910 for the express purpose of establishing a library. They called on "every lady in Hardin" to help with the project, as a "library would meet a long-felt need and would be a benefit to every man, woman and child in our community." The group immediately set out to raise funds. They hosted lectures, musical concerts, and locally produced dramas on a regular basis, using the ticket money to purchase reading materials. They housed the collection first at the school, then at the residence of Walter E. Fearis, who also served as librarian. By 1913, the library held one thousand items, acquired through donations and membership fees.

The library association, led by Fearis, decided a request to Carnegie was the next logical step. *The Hardin Tribune* editors agreed: "Carnegie or not, Hardin must have a library for its boys and girls, its men and women, who yearn for the companionship of the world's great masters of literature." Fearis suggested that the city seek Carnegie

▲ Dedicated in 1919, the Big Horn County Carnegie library in Hardin was designed in the Neoclassical Revival style by Billings architect C. L. Pruett. The rectangular red-brick building featured a full-height recessed central entry set off by Ionic columns and topped with a stepped-brick parapet. IMAGE COURTESY MONTANA HISTORICAL SOCIETY, 948-151.

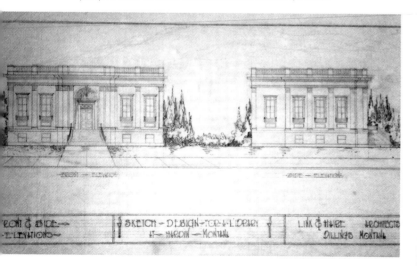

▲ The original design for the Hardin Carnegie library was more regal than the construction budget allowed.

funding for a library, pointing out that Hardin could use a facility similar to the one at Big Timber. He noted the urgent need for a building: the community had four saloons, one church, and many bad influences for its young men. The city of Hardin, including Mayor A. L. Mitchell and City Clerk F. M. Lipp, made the official application the following year.

At first, Bertram rejected the city's request for $10,000; the population was insufficient to justify the investment. In June 1915, he suggested that Big Horn County apply instead. Distrustful of the county's ability to administer a library, Fearis objected. He complained that Carnegie had granted a library to the "dead town" of Big Timber while refusing one to the growing town of Hardin. When Bertram remained steadfast in his decision, Fearis called on many influential people, including Montana Governor Sam V. Stewart and Senator Henry L. Myers, to help make his case.

Fearis's campaign worked, and Bertram offered Hardin $7,500 for a library building. Since this amount was not sufficient to build the needed space, additional negotiations ensured. Eventually Fearis agreed to create a county library, and with the support and advice of university librarian Gertrude Buckhous, the Carnegie Corporation offered a grant of $15,000.

Promise in hand, the county building committee set to work searching for an architect, securing the building lots, and ensuring the half-mill levy for library maintenance. They acquired two lots at the corner of Fifth Street and Custer Avenue, one purchased by local citizens and the other, by the Hardin Women's Club. Billings-based architect C. L. Pruett won the design contract, and after much negotiation, Bertram approved the plans in January 1918. Construction on the Neoclassical Revival building, performed by Percy Wilcox's company, commenced in April.

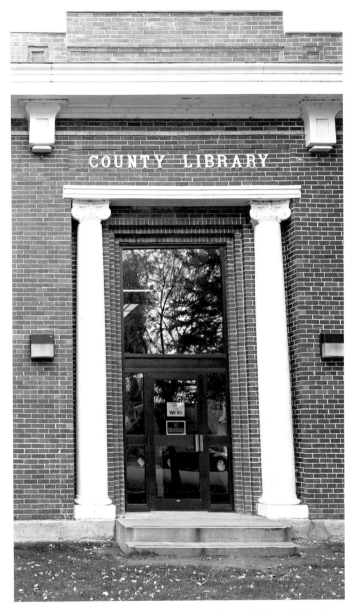

▲ C. L. Pruett designed a Neoclassical Revival Carnegie library in Hardin, featuring red brick walls, a recessed entry, and white Ionic columns.

COUNTY LIBRARY

▲ The Big Horn County Library has a long tradition of children's programming. Hardin residents Mrs. Holland and Mrs. James host a story hour party, ca. 1954. IMAGE COURTESY MONTANA HISTORICAL SOCIETY, PAC 2002-3 B1

▲ The children's area in the original daylight basement of the Bighorn County Carnegie library has plenty of floor space for activities.

Pruett distinguished the red-brick library with a full-height recessed central entry set off by Ionic columns and topped with a stepped parapet. He drew a deep, bracketed cornice around the roof and added sandstone accents.

Dedicated on June 22, 1919, with great fanfare, the new Big Horn County Library included spaces for adult and children's collections, a central foyer and circulation desk, and reading rooms. Two months later, Fearis reported to Bertram that the library's circulation had doubled and the public was making good use of the building. By 1926, the collection had grown to more than seven thousand volumes and circulation had surpassed twenty-five thousand. But through the 1920s, Big Horn County itself grew only modestly, forcing the library to rely on donations from the Hardin Women's Club.

In 1926, seventy-year-old Fearis retired, and Hazel Rennie Christiansen began her long career at the Big Horn County Library. Christiansen immediately began to expand service to the branches, including facilities at Crow Agency, Wyola, Kirby, Decker, St. Xavier, and Lodge Grass. She traveled the county regularly, and "took a very personal touch of the library to the many library borrowers over the county" until 1951, when she and her husband moved. In 1966, together with Yellowstone and Carbon Counties, Big Horn formed the South Central Library Federation, which allowed for greater cooperation between services and included eleven counties by 1976.

As happened with other Carnegie libraries across the state, the 1980s introduced more diversified collection and service possibilities, and in 1987 the library underwent a major expansion. The modern addition to the east side of the original building more than doubled its usable space and introduced a new, more accessible entrance from the south side. These developments coincided with an increase of services, including computers, multimedia collections, and additional programming and community meeting space. Big Horn County Library continues to be a strong cultural, social, and educational institution, serving as a gathering space and information hub for both Hardin and the county as a whole.

▲ The 1987 addition featured an accessible entrance and enlarged interior space, the new brick blending nicely with the original structure.

▲ In Bighorn County, the local Masons society served as the literal and figurative cornerstones of support for the Carnegie library.

RED LODGE

For centuries, the Apsáalooke (Crow) people occupied a vast territory in what would become southeast and south central Montana and northern Wyoming. Though the 1851 Fort Laramie Treaty reserved a large swath of the Crow's traditional land, subsequent decades witnessed treaties that far reduced the reservation. The 1880 agreement, ratified in 1882 and confirmed in 1892, included relinquishment of a "ceded strip" that included Biliíliikasshe, later named Rock Creek, to non-Indian settlement. Many of these settlers prized the area not only for its spectacular beauty but also for its lucrative coal beds.

The Rocky Fork Coal Company began its Red Lodge extraction activities in earnest after 1887. The Northern Pacific Railway branch line that arrived in 1890 brought immigrants from many European nations—Finns, English, Irish, Germans, Italians, Slavs—as well as European Americans to work in the mines. The growing multi-cultural community boasted numerous clubs and social groups, including a chapter of the Woman's Christian Temperance Union (WCTU), which espoused multiple social causes. Public libraries offered an alcohol-free recreation alternative as well as opportunities for education and social uplift. The Red Lodge WCTU members opened a reading room in November 1891. In addition to reading material, attentive volunteers provided "superb Java coffee and angel cake" to entice visitors. In 1900, the Red Lodge Miners Union collected $300 for library purposes, and a petition to establish a library and a one-mill levy to support it went before the city council, but the proposed levy did not pass the public vote.

Efforts to establish a free public library continued over the next decade. J. A. Metcalf, editor of the *Red Lodge Picket*, wrote to Andrew Carnegie, inquiring whether Red Lodge's "up-to-date progressive citizenship" might benefit

▲ Billings architect Warren A. Dedrick designed the Red Lodge Carnegie Library in 1918 and finished it in 1920, with hints of the Neoclassical Revival style. The addition to the rear was constructed in 1992 to provide much-needed space and technological amenities.

▲ As in most Montana communities, women were instrumental in garnering support and organizing community efforts to fund and build the Red Lodge Carnegie Library.

from his largess. Carnegie declined. Nine years later, the *Carbon County Journal* took up the cause, asking Red Lodge's residents, "Would it not be wise for this city to pause in its wild race for commercial and industrial development and consider the harvest which inevitably follows when such matters as providing clean and inspiring environment and recreation for the younger generation are neglected? . . . Do parents of this city wish their offspring to be confined to ignorance, hampered by degenerative influences, and robbed of elevating pastime?"

In 1913, the Women's Club of Red Lodge, with the assistance of the city clerk and *Picket* editor Walter Alderson, again wrote to Carnegie about funding a library. Popular sentiment favored a city library, and the city council assented to a levy and the purchase of a building site. Carnegie Corporation Secretary James Bertram responded with a $15,000 offer on June 11, 1914, though by then a newly elected city council determined that the levy question required a vote by property owners in the city. The women's club did not give up, campaigning for the levy until it passed in April 1917. Meanwhile, the city set up an interim library at the Savoy Hotel downtown, supported by city-paid rent, donations, and volunteer hours from women's club members.

Finally, in March 1918, the library board secured a triangular lot opposite the railroad depot and hired Billings architect Warren A. Dedrick to design the building. Dedrick had no experience with library design but had drawn successful plans for schools in Billings and northern Wyoming. His inexperience, and Bertram's exacting requirements, resulted in a drawn-out approval process. Using Carnegie's floor plan A, he offered a Neoclassical Revival-inspired rectangular building of dark red brick, a single story set on a daylight basement. The restrained decorative elements nearly epitomized Bertram's ideal structure: patterned brickwork to articulate the water table, quoining, and flat arched windows. Highlighted by a fanlight over the entry and keystones and a stepped cornice, the design provided the essential hints of classicism and distinguished detail. On the interior, only a vaulted vestibule and oak trimmings interrupted the utilitarian, yet welcoming, open floor plan. The basement lecture space and bathrooms offered practical convenience.

Negotiations over the design were not the only cause for delay. In August 1918 the library board voted to put construction on hold for the duration of the war. The Carnegie Corporation halted its library gift program in response to the war as well, choosing to move forward only with previously promised gifts. Finally, the library board awarded the necessary construction contracts in May 1919, and the building neared completion by September. With little fanfare, the Red Lodge Carnegie Library opened on January 26, 1920.

The contentious nature of the library's construction reflected the community's larger disputes. By the time the Carnegie library opened in 1920, it had housed US Army troops sent to the city to quell unrest, and tensions between the mine owners, unions, and political factions were high. Motivated by a five-month miners' strike in 1922 and the escalating cost of production, the Northern Pacific closed its Red Lodge mines in 1924. Though smaller mining interests continued in the area for the next

▲ The Red Lodge Carnegie Library continues to honor its rich legacy.

several decades, the population dropped by one-third between 1920 and 1930 and continued its decline through 1970. The loss of industry and population translated into a substantial loss of tax revenue, which led to decades of budget concerns for the library. Despite these misfortunes, librarian Mary Adams persevered throughout her forty-year tenure between 1925 and 1965.

The 1960s offered new opportunities for library management in Montana, and Adams's adopted son, assistant librarian Bob Moran, participated in discussions of countywide library services in 1962. After he assumed his mother's duties as head librarian in 1965, Moran worked with libraries in Bridger and Joliet to join the newly formed South Central Library Federation in 1970. Familiar

▲ The Red Lodge Carnegie Library features oak-trimmed fanlights which provide a beautiful focal point in the historic space.

budgetary concerns led to contentious negotiations between the Carbon County library board and the federation over the next several years.

The early 1990s began a Red Lodge renaissance when it was rediscovered for its recreational enticements, and the population slowly began to rise. This era coincided with a generous bequest to the library upon the death of Herbert Koski, a member of a longtime local Finnish family. The Koski donation funded a stylistically sympathetic addition to the rear of the library that improved access, doubled the square footage, and permitted technical upgrades. Audiobooks and video collections were introduced, but Moran noted that Red Lodge's patrons remained dedicated to the printed word: "We keep hearing forecasts, that books will become obsolete. . . . But I think that's a long way off. People are still readers." Moran retired in 2005,

ending the eighty-year reign of the Adams-Moran family at the Red Lodge Carnegie Library.

Following Moran's exit, the city of Red Lodge hired professional librarian Jodie Moore as library director and took steps to introduce improved services. Looking forward, the Red Lodge Carnegie Library remains intent on providing modern programming and access to information while respecting and preserving its own history. The library staff and trustees are committed to its mission to "engage our community with 21st Century materials, services, and technology to enhance literacy, civic, educational, and cultural opportunities." For nearly a century, the community has rallied for and embraced its dignified library building and the services it provides. Red Lodge will undoubtedly celebrate its Carnegie library for many decades to come.

▲ The Red Lodge Carnegie Library functions as a modern public library, while echoes of its historic past remain very much in evidence.

CHINOOK

Not long after the first trains pulled through the Milk River Valley in 1887, the community of Chinook sprang up along the tracks. By 1900, Chinook reported 1,586 residents, including railroad workers, sheep and cattle ranchers, and businessmen. Thousands more arrived in the area in the subsequent decade, fueled by railroad propaganda, the Enlarged Homestead Act, innovations in dryland farming, and the promise of irrigation via the ambitious Milk River Project. In 1912, lawmakers divided enormous Chouteau County into smaller jurisdictions, creating Blaine County, with Chinook as its county seat.

Members of the Women's Study Club in Chinook wrote to the Carnegie Corporation in 1916, inquiring about funding for a library. Carnegie Corporation Secretary James Bertram wrote back with instructions to secure a building site and revenue stream to support library maintenance. The women's club set to work, obtaining a donation of building lots from local businessman George Putnam. The group then canvassed the county, collecting signatures on a petition to place the library tax question on the fall election ballot. The club members persevered despite setbacks: "I became weary . . . tired in mind and body; each refusal caused all of us to become more depressed. . . . But we were still a determined bunch of women and would not give up. I am sure we trudged many miles during those last few days before the deadline, but we ended with our percentage of names . . . and we had a few names to spare."

The referendum passed in November 1916, but progress bogged down in confusion over population numbers. Finally, in October 1918, the Carnegie Corporation approved Blaine County's application for $15,000, and the project moved on to the design phase.

The county commissioners chose Havre architect

▲ George E. Ellinger's stripped-down Neoclassical Revival design for the Blaine County Carnegie library in Chinook in 1919 featured blond Hebron brick exterior walls, a centered entry with a decorative cornice, deep eaves, and large tripled windows. IMAGE COURTESY BLAINE COUNTY PUBLIC LIBRARY.

▲ Chinook school children gather for snacks on the steps of the Blaine County Carnegie library, ca. 1960. IMAGE COURTESY MONTANA HISTORICAL SOCIETY, PAC 2002-3 BI.

George E. Ellinger's bid on February 8, 1919. Chinook's library was Ellinger's first and only foray into Carnegie library design. Bertram rejected his first pair of offerings, judging the first out of proportion and noting that the second "could not have gone more contrary to the type plan." Though the county wished for a library comparable in size and elegance to those in Fort Benton, Malta, and Havre, construction costs had increased significantly by 1919.

Ellinger proceeded, fine-tuning the plans to accommodate the Carnegie Corporation's expectations and a restrictive budget. His dignified Neoclassical Revival design of one story on a daylight basement offered little decorative excess but managed the balanced fenestration, pilastered entry topped with a dentiled cornice, and deep eaves appropriate to the style. Constructed of blond Hebron brick, the hip-roofed building's large tripled

windows punctuated the façade, while smaller windows provided light from the side and rear elevations. Soldier-coursed brick added additional interest at the sills, water table, and roof line. The interior floor plan followed the Carnegie Corporation's "Plan B," with a central vestibule opening to the circulation desk and adult and children's reading rooms to either side. A lecture hall/clubroom occupied most of the basement level, sharing the space with bathrooms, an office, and a boiler room.

Bertram approved the plans in May 1919 and the balance of the paperwork four months later. Though the county hired a local experienced contractor, Maurice Montgomery, in early September, finishing the building proved challenging and time-consuming. County Clerk Vernon Butler explained to Bertram that the library remained unoccupied in March 1921, as the county could not afford to install the lighting fixtures. He assured Bertram that with the help of the women's club and other interested parties, the job would be complete "in the very near future." Indeed, the building's construction schedule coincided with exceedingly dry years and the collapse of much of Montana's agricultural economy. Because the farmers could not reap sufficient crops to make a living, taxes went delinquent, and the county's revenues plummeted. Book donations and library fundraisers, most often spearheaded by the women's club, facilitated the library's completion. The county hired professional librarian Patience Kemps (sometimes spelled Kemp), who arrived in late September 1921, and Blaine County Library officially opened in January 1922.

Community members soon began to use the Carnegie library in earnest. Most satisfied were George Putnam, who had donated the lots, and the women's club members, who held regular meetings in the library's basement room: "Mr. Putnam took great pride in watching the progress . . . he felt that he had been able to do something for his community that would be of lasting benefit to young and old alike. . . . The Club acted only as a representative of the community. . . . The community as a whole working together was responsible for our LIBRARY, of which we may all be justly proud."

Librarian Kemps cataloged not only the collection at the county library but also those at the school libraries in Chinook and Harlem. She participated in meetings of the Montana Library Association, taught library science, gave lectures, and attended social events to promote library services. Kemps left in 1923, and several different librarians took the helm over the next few years, during which time the library became an important "resource center for most of the students and adults in the county." Catherine O'Brien

▲ Interior stairs lead to the Blaine County library's original daylight basement.

▲ Vestiges of the Carnegie's "Floor Plan B," calling for a central vestibule opening to the circulation desk, with reading rooms on either side, are still evident in the Bear Paw Cooperative's office space in the former Carnegie library in Chinook.

took the job in 1927 and served the community in that capacity for forty years. Through the lean years of the 1930s, she organized book drives to keep the collection growing. By the 1940s, the library space, which was confined to the building's main floor, had become overcrowded. In 1957, O'Brien transformed the basement for use as a children's library and a research room. Particularly attentive to youthful patrons, each summer O'Brien would "entertain . . . all children who would enter school for the first time. She show[ed] them through the library, explaining . . . how they [could] use the library for pleasure and learning."

After O'Brien retired in 1967, Leona Jensen became the Blaine County librarian. Services continued to expand under Jensen's tenure, particularly after the library joined the newly formed Pathfinder Federation of Libraries in 1973. This consortium of central Montana libraries allowed for bookmobile and interlibrary loan capabilities as well as access to state and federal funding. The library took full advantage of the Library Services and Construction Act grant offerings, using the money to construct two new library buildings, one in Harlem in 1975 and another in Chinook in 1976. Opened in March 1976, the modern library in Chinook offered improved access, the capacity to grow the collections, and comfortable spaces. Over the next forty years, library programs continued to be modernized and to extend their reach across the county with improved technology, children's programming, and adult education.

When making plans for the new building during the early 1970s, the county considered demolishing the Carnegie library and building on the same lots. County commissioners cited the building's defects, including a condemned heating system, poor accessibility, and overcrowding. Fortunately, a larger building site just a few blocks away became available, and the historic library

▲ After the public library relocated in 1976, much of the Carnegie library was altered, though some original details remain.

remained in place and found other uses. Since that time, numerous county offices and groups have occupied the building, most recently the Bear Paw Cooperative, a nonprofit educational organization that serves North Central Montana. Though Ellinger's design has suffered some changes, including infilled windows and security doors, the essence of the building stands true. The tidy tan-brick edifice facing the county courthouse continues to proudly display "CARNEGIE LIBRARY" above its front door.

CONTRIBUTORS

Jamie Ford

Jamie Ford is the New York Times bestselling author of *Hotel on the Corner of Bitter and Sweet*, *Songs of Willow Frost*, and *Love and Other Consolation Prizes*. He is an avid public library patron and advocate, and lives in Great Falls, Montana.

Kate Hampton

Kate Hampton is the Community Preservation Officer at the Montana Historical Society's State Historic Preservation Office, where she also directs the award-winning "Identifying Montana's African-American Heritage Resources" project. Kate has authored numerous articles, presentations, and National Register nominations documenting Montana's historic built environment.

Tom Ferris

Tom Ferris has worked as an archival photographer at the Montana Historical Society for over two decades, and is the photographer of the books *Hand Raised: The Barns of Montana* and *Montana's Charlie Russell*. His work has also been exhibited in numerous galleries around Montana and in *Big Sky Journal*. More of Tom's work can be seen at www.tomferris.com.

SELECTED BIBLIOGRAPHY

Citations and a complete bibliography available from the author and the Montana History Foundation.

◼ Architectural Drawings

Bakke, Ole. "Missoula Carnegie Library Addition." 1913. Architectural Drawings. Gibson, Kirkemo, and Bakke Architectural Drawings, 1890-1971. Mss 020, Series XXVII: Missoula, Montana, Set 16b. Missoula, MT: Archives and Special Collections, Maureen and Mike Mansfield Library, University of Montana.

Cohagen, Chandler C. "Lewistown Carnegie Public Library Busch Memorial Addition." August – October 1958. Architectural Drawings. Collection Number 2086, Drawing Set 308, Montana State University-Bozeman Library, Merrill G. Burlingame Special Collections (hereafter MSU-Bozeman).

Haire, Charles S. Architectural Drawings for Bozeman and Miles City Carnegie Libraries. Collection Number 863, Drawing Sets 330 and 199, MSU-Bozeman.

Haire, Charles S. Architectural Drawings for Dillon and Great Falls Carnegie Libraries. Collection Number 2040, Drawing Sets 103 and 306, MSU-Bozeman.

Link & Haire, Architects. "Big Timber Carnegie Library." May 8, 1913. Architectural Drawings. Collection Number 1130, Drawing Set 013, MSU-Bozeman.

◼ Newspapers

Anaconda Standard, Big Timber Pioneer, Billings Gazette, Bozeman Avant-Courier, Bozeman Daily Chronicle, Bozeman Weekly Chronicle, Butte Daily Post, Butte Intermountain, Carbon County Journal [Red Lodge], *Choteau Acantha, Conrad Independent, Daily Inter Lake* [Kalispell], *Daily Missoulian, Daily News* [Havre], *Dillon Tribune, Dillon Examiner, Enterprise* [Malta], *Fergus County Argus* [Lewistown], *Fergus County Democrat* [Lewistown], *Glasgow Courier, Great Falls Daily Tribune, Great Falls Leader, Great Falls Tribune, Great Falls Weekly Tribune, The Hardin Tribune, Hardin Tribune-Herald, Havre Daily News, Helena Weekly Herald, Independent Record* [Helena], *The Inland Empire* [Moore], *Kalispell Bee, Livingston Enterprise, Milk River Eagle, Missoulian, Montana Standard* [Butte], *Phillips County News* [Malta], *Pickett-Journal* [Red Lodge], *Red Lodge Picket, River Press* [Fort Benton], *Rosebud County News* [Forsyth], *Tribune-Examiner* [Dillon], *Western News* [Stevensville], *Wibaux Pioneer, Yellowstone Journal* [Miles City]

◼ Books, Articles, Collections, and Manuscripts

Anonymous. "Public Buildings." Vol. 35, No. 21. (October 19, 1907) *Improvement Bulletin.* Minneapolis: Chapin Publishing Company.

Anonymous. "Resolution Honoring Bonnie Williamson, Retiring Library Director, Havre-Hill County Library." Helena, MT: Montana State Library Commission, 2012.

Badger Doyle, Susan, Ed. *Journey to the Land of Gold: Emigrant Diaries from the Bozeman Trail, 1863-1866.* Vol. 1. Helena, MT: MHS Press, 2000.

Brock, Linda Dale. "Carnegie Libraries in Montana: Private Building as Form, Function, and Story." 83rd ACSA Annual Meeting, History/Theory/Criticism, 1995.

Buckhous, Gertrude. "The County Library." *University of Montana Bulletin.* No. 13. (March 1918) Missoula, MT: State University Series.

Carnegie Corporation of New York Records, 1872-2000. Series II: Files on Microfilm, ca. 1866-1977, II.A: Gifts and Grants, II.A.1: Libraries, II.A.1.a. Free Public Library Buildings, Reels 3-26. New York: Columbia University Rare Book and Manuscript Library.

Carnegie Corporation of New York. "Notes on the Erection of Library Bildings." [*sic*] Revised 1918. Pittsburgh, PA: Carnegie Mellon University Andrew Carnegie Online Archives.

Chacon, Hipolito Rafael. *The Original Man: The Life and Work of Architect A.J. Gibson.* Missoula, MT: University of Montana Press and Montana Museum of Art and Culture, 2008.

Clayton, John. *Images of America: Red Lodge.* Arcadia Publishing, 2008.

Connelly, Phil. "Bitterroot Public Library History." 2018. Unpublished timeline. On file at the Bitterroot Public Library.

Curry, Jim. *Parmly Billings Library: The First Hundred Years.* Billings, MT: Parmly Billings Library, 2002.

Dean, Patty. "LaGrande Cannon Boulevard National Register of Historic Places (hereafter NR) Nomination." 2013. Draft on file at Montana State Historic Preservation Office, Helena, MT (hereafter MTSHPO).

DeCruyen, Lisa. "The History and Development of Rural Public Libraries." Spring 1980. *Library Trends*.

DeHaas, John. "Bozeman Carnegie Library NR Nomination." February 1979. On file at MTSHPO.

DeHaas, John. "Dillon City Library NR Nomination." October 1978. On file at MTSHPO.

Haley, Josephine M. "Montana Library Association Report." Vol. 18, No. 1. (January 1918) *Public Libraries*. Chicago: Library Bureau.

Hampton, Kate and Lauren McMullen. "Big Timber Carnegie Library NR Nomination." 2002. On file at MTSHPO.

Hanshew, Annie. "Alma Smith Jacobs: Beloved Librarian, Tireless Activist." In *Beyond Schoolmarms and Madams: Montana Women's Stories*, edited by Martha Kohl. Helena, MT: MHS Press, 2016.

Hill, Frank Pierce. *James Bertram: An Appreciation*. New York: Carnegie Corporation of New York, 1936.

History Committee of the Pioneer Museum. *Footprints in the Valley: A History of Valley County, Montana*. Glasgow, MT: Glasgow Courier & Printing, 1991.

Hughes, John and Anna Zellick. "Lewistown Carnegie Library NR Nomination." 1979. On file at MT SHPO.

Jenks, Jim. *A Guide to Historic Bozeman*. Helena, MT: MHS Press, 2007.

Jensen, Leona. "History of the Blaine County Library." 1976. Unpublished essay. On file at the Blaine County Library, Chinook, MT.

Kettering, Florence. "Lewistown Public Library." c. 1985. Unpublished essay. On file at Lewistown Public Library.

Kuhlman, Erika A. "From Farmland to Coalvillage: Red Lodge's Finnish Immigrants, 1890-1922." 1987. Master's Thesis. Missoula, MT: University of Montana Department of History.

Leavengood, David. "Livingston Commercial Historic District NR Nomination." June 1979. On file at MTSHPO.

Long, Samantha. "Establishing the Red Lodge Carnegie Library." 2018. Unpublished timeline. On file at the Carbon County Historical Society and Museum, Red Lodge, MT.

McKay, Kathy. "Montana Historical and Architectural Inventory 1992 Revision: 302 Second Avenue East." 1992. On file at MTSHPO.

McKay, Kathy. "Historic and Architectural Properties of Kalispell, Montana NR Multiple Properties Documentation Form." June 1993. On file at MTSHPO.

Michaels, Kirk and Ada Powell. "Montana Historical and Architectural Inventory, 312 State Street, Hamilton Commercial Historic District." 1987. On file at MTSHPO.

Montana State Legislature. "An Act to Provide for the Establishment of Free Libraries." 1883 Territorial Laws of Montana 110-111.

Montana State Legislature. "An Act to Provide for Library Extension through the Establishment and Maintenance of County Free libraries." Chapter 45, Montana Laws 1915, p. 64.

Pasma, Hazel Allison. "Story of Blaine County Library." 1955. Unpublished article. On file at the Blaine County Library, Chinook, MT.

Quivik, Fred L. "Historic Resources of Hardin, Montana NR Multiple Resource Area Documentation." September 1984. On file at MTSHPO.

Ring, Daniel F. "Carnegie Libraries as Symbols for an Age: Montana As a Test Case." Vol. 27, No. 1. (Winter 1992) *Library and Culture*.

S. Jeanne. Memorial essays for Laura Manderscheid Brown Zook, Mildred George Myers Schlosser, and Muriel Josephine Dahlin Cooksey. On *Find A Grave* website.

Sedlacek, Signe M. Chair. *Grit, Guts, and Gusto*. Havre, MT: Hill County Bicentennial Commission, 1976.

Smith, Clare M. "Miles City Carnegie Public Library: 1902-1968." April 1968. *The Montana Woman*.

Spritzer, Don. *Roadside History of Montana*. Missoula, MT: Mountain Press, 1999.

Swetnam, Susan H. *Books, Bluster, & Bounty: Local Politics and Intermountain West Carnegie Library Building Grants, 1898-1920*. Logan, Utah: Utah State University Press, 2012.

Taylor, Linda and Michael Koop. "[Chouteau County] Carnegie Public Library NR Nomination." 1986. On file at MTSHPO.

Van Slyck, Abigail A. *Free to All: Carnegie Libraries & American Culture: 1890-1920*. Chicago: University of Chicago Press, 1995.

West, Carroll Van. "Thomas Molesworth and the Western Room at the Glasgow Library." *Montana's Historic Landscapes* website.

Wiegand, Wayne A. *Part of Our Lives: A People's History of the American Public Library*. London: Oxford University Press, 2015.